WebAssembly in Rust

A Developer's Guide to High-Performance
Web Programming with Safe Systems Code

Jose Gobert

Copyright Page

Table of Contents

Preface 5

Chapter 1: Introducing WebAssembly and Rust 7

What is WebAssembly 7

Benefits of Using Rust with WebAssembly 8

Use Cases: Performance-Critical Web Apps, Portability, and Safety
....10

Overview of the Development and Deployment Flow 11

Chapter 2: Setting Up Your Rust and Wasm Development Environment
....14

Installing Rust and wasm-pack 14

Using `cargo-generate` and Project Templates............................17

Building Your First Wasm Project in Rust.......................................19

Using `wasm-pack` with npm and Bundlers.................................. 22

Chapter 3: Writing Rust for WebAssembly 26

Restrictions of the Wasm Execution Environment 26

Working Within `no_std` Limitations.. 29

Understanding wasm-bindgen, web-sys, and js-sys......................... 32

Memory Safety and Cross-Language Interop 36

Chapter 4: Calling JavaScript from Rust and Vice Versa 42

Bridging Rust and JavaScript... 42

Bridging Rust and JavaScript... 47

Working with `JsValue` and Type Conversions.............................51

Handling Events and Callbacks.. 56

Passing Complex Data Structures Across the Boundary 62

Chapter 5: Building Real Web Interfaces with Rust and Wasm......... 69

DOM Manipulation Using Rust 69

Using `web-sys` to Access Browser APIs... 74

Creating a Simple Interactive Frontend.. 80

Integrating with JavaScript Frameworks.. 85

Chapter 6: Performance Optimization in Rust-Wasm Apps 91

Memory Layout and Allocation Strategies 91

Optimizing Binary Size with `wasm-opt` 95

Avoiding Unnecessary Bindings 99

Benchmarking Rust and JavaScript 105

Chapter 7: Real-World Application Case Study 111

Building a Full Web App (Markdown Converter) 111

Project Structure and Module Organization 116

Packaging for Deployment 121

Comparing Performance Gains 125

Chapter 8: Testing and Debugging Rust-Wasm Code 130

Unit Testing with `wasm-bindgen-test` 130

Debugging Rust in the Browser 134

Logging, Error Handling, and Diagnostics 140

Interoperability Test Strategies 145

Chapter 9: Deploying Rust-Wasm to Production 152

Hosting Options (Static Site, CDN, Serverless) 157
Best Practices for Loading and Caching WebAssembly (Wasm) ... 162

CI/CD Pipelines for Rust-Wasm Workflows 167

Chapter 10: Beyond the Browser: WASI and Server-Side WebAssembly
.... 173

Introduction to WASI (WebAssembly System Interface) 173

Running Rust-Wasm on the Backend 177

Tauri and Cross-Platform Desktop Apps 181

The Future of WebAssembly Beyond Frontend 185

Appendices 190

Preface

The web has evolved into a powerful platform capable of running high-performance applications, traditionally the domain of native desktop software. Yet, despite advances in JavaScript engines and frameworks, web developers still encounter challenges when building compute-intensive features such as real-time image processing, simulation engines, or data manipulation tools. This is where **WebAssembly (Wasm)** comes in.

WebAssembly is a low-level, binary instruction format designed to run alongside JavaScript in modern browsers at near-native speed. It provides a compilation target for languages like C, C++, and **Rust**, allowing developers to run highly optimized, memory-efficient code directly in the browser.

This book focuses on programming WebAssembly with **Rust**, a systems programming language known for its performance, safety, and reliability. Rust is particularly well-suited for WebAssembly due to its strong guarantees around memory safety and its powerful compiler optimizations. When compiled to Wasm, Rust enables developers to build fast and secure web applications without sacrificing developer experience or maintainability.

The purpose of this book is to teach you how to create **high-performance web applications using Rust and WebAssembly**, in a way that is practical, focused, and grounded in real-world use cases. Whether you're a seasoned Rust developer looking to target the web, or a web developer eager to break through JavaScript's performance ceiling, this book will provide you with the skills you need to succeed.

This book is written for several types of readers:

- **Rust developers** who want to explore how their code can run in the browser through WebAssembly.
- **Web developers** who are seeking performance and control beyond what JavaScript can provide.
- **System programmers and tool builders** who want to leverage WebAssembly as a deployment target for cross-platform web-based tools.
- **Students and professionals** who are curious about the growing role of Wasm in frontend, backend, and edge computing.

No prior experience with WebAssembly is required, but a working understanding of Rust and JavaScript will help you get the most out of the content. Each chapter builds on the previous one, moving from foundational concepts to practical application, testing, optimization, and deployment. Key terms like `wasm-bindgen`, `web-sys`, and `wasm-pack` are introduced carefully and used with examples to illustrate how they contribute to the Rust-to-Wasm toolchain.

Throughout the book, you'll work through real examples—building modules that interact with JavaScript, manipulate the DOM, handle memory efficiently, and produce meaningful performance gains. The goal is not just to demonstrate what is possible, but to help you develop an instinct for writing maintainable, production-ready Rust code that targets the web.

If you are looking to create fast, reliable, and secure web applications that go beyond traditional limitations, then this book will give you the knowledge and confidence to do so. You'll leave not only with a solid grasp of how WebAssembly works with Rust, but also with practical insight into how to apply it effectively in modern web development.

Let's begin by understanding what WebAssembly is, and why Rust is the ideal language for writing it.

Chapter 1: Introducing WebAssembly and Rust

What is WebAssembly

WebAssembly, commonly referred to as **Wasm**, is a low-level binary instruction format that runs in web browsers. It is designed to be a **portable compilation target** for high-level programming languages like Rust, C, and C++. This means that instead of writing applications in JavaScript alone, developers can write performance-critical components in a language like Rust, compile that code to WebAssembly, and then run it directly in the browser with near-native speed.

Unlike JavaScript, which is interpreted or just-in-time compiled, WebAssembly is **compiled ahead of time (AOT)** into a binary format that is fast to download, parse, and execute. This gives WebAssembly a significant performance advantage, particularly for compute-intensive tasks such as graphics rendering, real-time data processing, or cryptographic calculations.

WebAssembly was created to address some of the long-standing limitations of the traditional web stack. Although JavaScript has evolved dramatically and powers the majority of modern web applications, it wasn't originally designed with performance-critical use cases in mind. Operations that require manual memory management, direct access to system-level APIs, or predictable execution times can be difficult to achieve reliably in JavaScript. This is where WebAssembly provides a meaningful improvement.

One of the most important aspects of WebAssembly is its **sandboxed execution model**. Code compiled to Wasm runs in a tightly controlled environment with no direct access to the host machine's memory or operating system. This makes it a **secure** option for running third-party modules or computational logic in the browser without risking system compromise. WebAssembly is also **platform-independent**, meaning that a single binary can run consistently across different devices, browsers, and operating systems.

The Wasm specification is designed with performance, safety, and efficiency in mind. It includes a structured stack-based execution model, a compact binary format, and deterministic behavior. These characteristics make it well-suited not only for the browser but also for emerging areas like **server-side computing**, **IoT**, and **edge applications**.

WebAssembly is not intended to replace JavaScript but rather to **complement it**. In a typical modern application, JavaScript still handles tasks like user interface updates, event handling, and DOM manipulation, while WebAssembly takes over performance-critical logic. They operate side by side, with WebAssembly modules being loaded by JavaScript and invoked as needed.

In practice, this hybrid model allows developers to **push the limits of what web applications can do**. By offloading computation-heavy parts of an app—such as image processing, data compression, or game logic—into a WebAssembly module, you can significantly improve performance while still maintaining the flexibility and convenience of the traditional web stack.

WebAssembly matters because it **extends the capabilities of the web** in a way that is fast, secure, and open. It gives developers new options for solving performance challenges and enables entire classes of applications that were previously impractical to run inside a browser. With wide support across all major browsers and an actively growing ecosystem, WebAssembly has become a core part of the future of high-performance web development.

Benefits of Using Rust with WebAssembly

Rust is widely regarded as one of the best programming languages for compiling to WebAssembly, and for good reason. The language was designed from the ground up to provide both **high performance** and **strong safety guarantees**, making it an excellent match for the execution model and constraints of WebAssembly.

One of the most important benefits of using Rust with WebAssembly is **memory safety without garbage collection**. WebAssembly itself does not include a garbage collector like JavaScript or Java. This means that when targeting Wasm, developers must manage memory explicitly or rely on a language that provides deterministic memory management. Rust offers a powerful alternative through its ownership system. This system enforces strict rules at compile time about how memory is accessed and mutated, preventing issues like use-after-free, double-free, or null pointer dereferencing. The result is safe code that doesn't incur the runtime overhead of garbage collection.

Performance is another key area where Rust complements WebAssembly effectively. Rust compiles to highly optimized machine code, and when that code is translated to WebAssembly, it produces **compact, efficient binaries**. These binaries load quickly in the browser, use less memory, and execute faster than equivalent code written in JavaScript. Rust's lack of runtime overhead and predictable performance characteristics make it ideal for implementing features that require low latency, such as games, simulations, image processing, or real-time data analysis.

Rust also provides precise control over **low-level operations**, such as bitwise manipulation, buffer management, and system-like memory access. This level of control is essential for many WebAssembly use cases, where a developer might need to tightly manage data layout and performance tuning. At the same time, Rust's high-level abstractions, like pattern matching and trait-based generics, allow developers to write expressive and maintainable code without compromising on speed.

Interoperability between Rust and JavaScript is made easier by tools like `wasm-bindgen`, which enables seamless communication between Rust and the JavaScript environment. This allows developers to call JavaScript APIs from Rust and expose Rust functions to JavaScript with minimal effort. The `web-sys` crate further extends this capability by offering bindings to the browser's Web APIs—such as the DOM, Canvas, and Web Audio—so developers can build rich, interactive experiences without writing JavaScript for everything.

Another advantage of using Rust with WebAssembly is the robustness of the ecosystem. Tools like `wasm-pack` help automate the process of building, testing, and publishing WebAssembly packages written in Rust. These tools reduce the complexity of the workflow and make it easier to integrate Rust code into modern frontend build systems like Webpack, Vite, or Rollup.

Security is a foundational strength of both Rust and WebAssembly. Rust's compile-time checks eliminate many common sources of bugs and vulnerabilities, while WebAssembly's sandboxed execution ensures that compiled code cannot access resources outside of its defined boundaries. This combination significantly reduces the attack surface of web applications, making Rust-Wasm modules a safer choice for executing untrusted or performance-critical code.

Finally, because Rust is a systems-level language with first-class support for cross-compilation, code written in Rust and compiled to WebAssembly can often be reused across platforms. A Rust module might serve as the core logic in a web application, a desktop application using Tauri, and even a backend service using WASI or native binaries—allowing for consistency and reduced duplication across different environments.

Using Rust with WebAssembly gives developers the rare ability to write code that is **fast, safe, portable, and modern**, all at once. It unlocks the performance potential of the web while maintaining code clarity and long-term maintainability.

Use Cases: Performance-Critical Web Apps, Portability, and Safety

WebAssembly, particularly when combined with Rust, is well-suited for scenarios where performance, portability, and safety are top priorities. While many web applications can be built entirely with JavaScript and modern frameworks, there are specific cases where these technologies struggle to meet performance or safety requirements. In these situations, compiling Rust to WebAssembly provides a practical and efficient solution.

One of the most common use cases is in **performance-critical web applications**. These are applications that rely heavily on fast execution of complex logic, such as games, simulations, image or video processing tools, audio engines, or data analysis platforms. JavaScript can handle many tasks well, but when applications need to process large volumes of data, update graphics in real-time, or perform continuous calculations, the limitations of interpreted or just-in-time compiled code become more apparent. Rust, being a compiled systems language, generates WebAssembly code that executes much closer to native machine speed. This allows developers to move compute-heavy parts of their application into WebAssembly modules, achieving better frame rates, lower latency, and reduced CPU usage.

Another important benefit is **portability**. WebAssembly is a standardized binary format supported by all modern web browsers, and it runs consistently across platforms. This means developers can write application logic in Rust once, compile it to WebAssembly, and expect it to work identically in Chrome, Firefox, Safari, and Edge, regardless of the operating system. Unlike JavaScript, which may behave slightly differently across environments and engine versions, WebAssembly provides a stable and predictable execution environment. Beyond the browser, WebAssembly is also gaining traction in server-side runtimes like Wasmtime and Wasmer, and in edge platforms such as Cloudflare Workers. This allows the same compiled Rust-Wasm module to be deployed in the browser, on the server, and even in embedded systems, with no change to the source code.

Security and reliability are also key reasons to use Rust with WebAssembly. Applications that deal with user input, third-party extensions, or sensitive operations must be resilient against memory corruption, injection attacks, and undefined behavior. WebAssembly code executes inside a sandbox, isolated from the host system and limited to a defined set of capabilities. This ensures that even if a vulnerability exists, the potential for harm is significantly reduced. Rust further strengthens safety by enforcing strict rules around memory access and data ownership at compile time. This eliminates entire categories of bugs that are common in languages like C or C++, such as buffer overflows or use-after-free errors. As a result, developers can write high-performance modules that are both secure and robust.

A practical example of this is a web-based image editor. A typical implementation in JavaScript might suffer from slow filter processing on large images. By moving the filter logic into a Rust-based WebAssembly module, the same task can be completed much faster and with greater consistency across devices. Another example is a financial visualization tool that processes thousands of data points per second. Offloading the computation to WebAssembly helps reduce UI thread blocking and keeps the interface smooth and responsive.

These use cases highlight the versatility of combining Rust and WebAssembly. It is not about replacing JavaScript, but about extending what is possible in modern web applications. By focusing on performance, portability, and safety, developers gain more control over how their applications behave, scale, and respond to real-world usage. This approach is especially valuable in professional software development, where efficiency and correctness directly impact user experience and business outcomes.

Overview of the Development and Deployment Flow

Building applications with Rust and WebAssembly involves a specialized workflow that bridges systems programming and web development. To use Rust effectively in a WebAssembly context, it's important to understand how code is written, compiled, integrated with frontend environments, and deployed to production.

The development process typically begins with writing code in Rust using standard language features, along with additional tools and crates designed specifically for WebAssembly. Since WebAssembly has no direct access to the operating system, file system, or threads (in most browser environments), Rust code targeting Wasm must respect certain constraints. The Rust standard library is available in a limited form, and the focus is on writing `no_std`-compatible or Wasm-friendly logic that can execute safely and predictably inside the browser.

To build a Rust crate that compiles to WebAssembly, the Rust compiler (`rustc`) is used alongside a tool called `wasm-pack`. This toolchain simplifies the build process by compiling Rust code to a `.wasm` binary and generating the associated JavaScript bindings automatically. These bindings make it possible for JavaScript code in the browser to call Rust functions and for Rust code to call JavaScript APIs. Behind the scenes, `wasm-bindgen` is used to create glue code that handles type conversions and manages the communication between the two runtimes.

Once the `.wasm` module is generated, it can be bundled with JavaScript and other frontend assets using a bundler like Webpack, Rollup, or Vite. This step prepares the WebAssembly binary and the JavaScript wrapper for inclusion in a web application. During development, this integration allows for features like hot module replacement, live reloading, and debugging through browser dev tools. Developers can call Rust functions from JavaScript just like any other imported module, enabling tight integration with user interfaces, event listeners, and DOM manipulation.

As the application matures, performance and size become important considerations. The raw WebAssembly output may contain debug information or unoptimized sections that increase file size or slow down execution. To prepare for production, tools like `wasm-opt` from the Binaryen toolkit are used to reduce the size of the binary and improve execution efficiency. These optimizations are essential for reducing load time, especially on mobile networks or resource-constrained devices.

The final stage is deployment. WebAssembly binaries are served just like any other static asset—typically alongside HTML, CSS, and JavaScript files. A correctly configured web server should set the appropriate MIME type (`application/wasm`) for `.wasm` files so that browsers recognize and execute them properly. In most frontend projects, this means placing the `.wasm` and associated JS files into a `dist` or `build` directory and using standard hosting platforms or CDNs to distribute them to users.

Deployment environments vary depending on the type of application. For single-page applications, traditional static hosting services like Netlify, Vercel, or GitHub Pages are often sufficient. For more advanced use cases— such as apps running on the edge or server-side WebAssembly execution using WASI (WebAssembly System Interface)—deployment may involve specialized platforms like Cloudflare Workers, Fastly Compute@Edge, or Docker containers running Wasmtime.

Throughout this process, the Rust and WebAssembly toolchain provides strong support for testing, debugging, and packaging. Developers can write unit tests using `wasm-bindgen-test`, log errors to the browser console, and build reusable packages that can be published to npm or crates.io.

The development and deployment flow for Rust and WebAssembly includes writing Wasm-compatible Rust code, compiling it with `wasm-pack`, integrating the output into a frontend project, optimizing the final binary, and deploying it to a static host or dynamic runtime. Each step builds on well-supported tools and practices, making it practical for developers to produce fast, secure, and portable web applications with confidence.

Chapter 2: Setting Up Your Rust and Wasm Development Environment

Before you can build high-performance applications with Rust and WebAssembly, you need to set up a development environment that supports compiling Rust code to WebAssembly and integrating it into a web-based frontend. Fortunately, the Rust ecosystem has matured significantly in recent years, and there are powerful tools that make this process smoother and more consistent. In this chapter, you'll install the essential tools, scaffold a project using community-maintained templates, compile a working WebAssembly module, and prepare it for use in a JavaScript-based application.

Installing Rust and wasm-pack

Before you can begin building high-performance WebAssembly applications with Rust, you need to have the right tooling in place. In this section, I'll guide you step-by-step through installing the Rust programming language along with `wasm-pack`, which is the primary tool you'll use to compile Rust code into WebAssembly and prepare it for use in modern JavaScript applications. These tools are actively maintained by the Rust and WebAssembly communities, and they form the backbone of your development environment.

Let's begin with the Rust toolchain itself. Rust is distributed through a tool called `rustup`, which manages everything from compiler versions to target platforms. It makes it easy to keep your toolchain up to date and consistent across different machines or team members. To install it, run the following command in your terminal:

```
curl --proto '=https' --tlsv1.2 -sSf
https://sh.rustup.rs | sh
```

This script will download and install the latest stable version of Rust along with its package manager, `cargo`. During the installation, you'll be asked to confirm the default settings. Unless you have a specific reason to modify them, the defaults are usually the right choice. Once the installation completes, close and reopen your terminal (or source your shell profile), and verify that the tools were installed correctly:

```
rustc --version

cargo --version
```

You should see version numbers for both tools printed to the terminal. These indicate that Rust and Cargo are now available globally on your system. `rustc` is the Rust compiler, and `cargo` is the Rust build system and package manager that you'll use to compile your code and manage dependencies.

Next, you'll need to add the WebAssembly compilation target to your toolchain. Rust compiles to WebAssembly using a specific target called `wasm32-unknown-unknown`. This target represents a 32-bit WebAssembly environment without an operating system or standard system libraries, which matches the sandboxed nature of the web. To install the target, run:

```
rustup target add wasm32-unknown-unknown
```

This command tells the compiler that you intend to build Rust code for the WebAssembly platform, and it installs the necessary architecture support files.

Now let's move on to `wasm-pack`. This tool streamlines the entire process of building WebAssembly modules from Rust. It handles compilation, generates JavaScript bindings, and even prepares your module as an npm package so it can be published or consumed in a frontend project. To install `wasm-pack`, you can use Cargo directly:

```
cargo install wasm-pack
```

This may take a minute, as Cargo will compile the tool from source and install it into your local binary directory. Once it's done, confirm the installation:

```
wasm-pack --version
```

If everything is working correctly, you'll see the installed version of `wasm-pack` printed to the screen.

At this point, your system is fully equipped to build and run Rust-based WebAssembly applications. You have the Rust compiler for compiling source code, Cargo for managing dependencies and builds, the `wasm32-unknown-unknown` target for generating WebAssembly binaries, and `wasm-pack` for producing WebAssembly modules that integrate with modern JavaScript tooling.

Let's test your installation with a small practical exercise. Create a new Rust library project with:

```
cargo new --lib hello-wasm

cd hello-wasm
```

Then open the `Cargo.toml` file and add the following dependencies:

```
[lib]

crate-type = ["cdylib"]


[dependencies]

wasm-bindgen = "0.2"
```

This configuration tells Cargo to compile the library as a `cdylib`, which is required for WebAssembly output, and includes `wasm-bindgen`, which helps connect Rust functions to JavaScript.

Next, edit `src/lib.rs` and add a basic function:

```
use wasm_bindgen::prelude::*;

#[wasm_bindgen]
pub fn greet(name: &str) -> String {
    format!("Hello, {}!", name)
}
```

Now run the build:

```
wasm-pack build
```

This will compile your code into a `.wasm` binary and create a `pkg/` directory with all the JavaScript wrappers needed to use it in a web project.

This exercise demonstrates that your tools are working correctly and are capable of producing WebAssembly modules from Rust code. In the next section, we'll use project templates and automation tools to create more complex applications efficiently. For now, you've taken a critical first step in preparing your environment for real WebAssembly development with Rust.

Using `cargo-generate` and Project Templates

As you start building applications with Rust and WebAssembly, one of the first things you'll notice is that setting up a project from scratch can involve quite a bit of boilerplate. You'll need a proper directory layout, the right `Cargo.toml` configuration, and specific attributes like `#[wasm_bindgen]` in your source files. While you could certainly create this structure manually, there's a more efficient approach: use a template.

This is where `cargo-generate` comes in. It's a command-line tool that simplifies the process of scaffolding new Rust projects based on pre-configured templates. Instead of copying and pasting files or repeatedly creating the same folder structure, you can use `cargo-generate` to clone a remote template repository and customize it for your own use with a single command.

To get started, install the tool globally using Cargo:

```
cargo install cargo-generate
```

Once installed, you can verify that it's available on your system by running:

```
cargo generate --help
```

You should see a list of command options and flags. This confirms that you're ready to use the tool.

One of the most widely recommended templates for Rust WebAssembly development is maintained by the Rust WebAssembly Working Group. It's available at:

```
https://github.com/rustwasm/wasm-pack-template
```

This template includes everything you need to begin building and compiling a WebAssembly module in Rust, including the required crate configuration, build targets, and a sample function to test that everything works as expected.

Let's walk through creating a new project using this template. First, choose a name for your project—let's say you're building a simple math module—and then run:

```
cargo generate --git
https://github.com/rustwasm/wasm-pack-template --
name wasm-math
```

When you execute this command, `cargo-generate` will clone the template repository into a new folder named `wasm-math`, update internal references such as the crate name, and initialize a clean Git repository for you. Inside the new project folder, you'll see a structure like this:

```
wasm-math/
├── Cargo.toml
├── src/
│   └── lib.rs
├── README.md
```

The `Cargo.toml` file is already configured for compiling to WebAssembly. It sets the crate type to `cdylib`, which is required for Wasm output, and includes the `wasm-bindgen` dependency so that Rust functions can be called from JavaScript. The `src/lib.rs` file includes a basic example function:

```
use wasm_bindgen::prelude::*;

#[wasm_bindgen]
pub fn add(a: i32, b: i32) -> i32 {
    a + b
}
```

This function is public, exposed to JavaScript using the `#[wasm_bindgen]` attribute, and ready to compile into a `.wasm` module. You could now build this module with `wasm-pack build`, and it would output a WebAssembly binary and the corresponding JavaScript interface code in a `pkg/` directory.

The benefit of using a project template like this becomes more obvious as your applications grow. Instead of repeatedly configuring every new module by hand, you can rely on templates to ensure consistency and correctness. This is especially useful for teams working across multiple projects where a standardized project layout, consistent build scripts, and uniform metadata help reduce mistakes and improve collaboration.

You can also create your own custom templates for internal use. Suppose your organization builds multiple Rust-Wasm utilities that share common patterns—like certain dependencies, build flags, or test configurations—you could publish your own private template and use `cargo-generate` to scaffold new tools that follow your team's best practices.

To create a reusable template, start by creating a public or private Git repository that follows the standard layout. In the `Cargo.toml`, you can use placeholders like `{{project-name}}` and `{{authors}}`, which `cargo-generate` will automatically fill in when generating a new project. Add a `cargo-generate.toml` file to customize prompts or variable substitution.

By using templates in combination with `cargo-generate`, you save time, reduce setup errors, and ensure a smooth workflow from the first line of code to the final compiled WebAssembly module. It's one of those foundational practices that pays off every time you start a new project.

Building Your First Wasm Project in Rust

Now that you've installed Rust, added the WebAssembly compilation target, and generated a starter project using `cargo-generate`, you're ready to compile your first real WebAssembly module written in Rust. In this section, you'll walk through writing a basic Rust function, compiling it to `.wasm`, and preparing it for use in a web environment. You'll also learn how the `wasm-pack` toolchain works and what happens during the build process.

Start by navigating to the project directory you generated earlier—if you used the wasm-pack template and named it `wasm-math`, then:

```
cd wasm-math
```

Inside this project, open `src/lib.rs`. This is the main entry point for your library. You'll find a default function there—usually a simple arithmetic or greeting function wrapped in the `#[wasm_bindgen]` attribute. Let's start fresh and replace its contents with something straightforward and useful.

Here's a basic example that exposes a function to square a number:

```
use wasm_bindgen::prelude::*;

/// Squares an integer and returns the result
```

```
#[wasm_bindgen]
pub fn square(n: i32) -> i32 {
    n * n
}
```

This function takes an i32 value, multiplies it by itself, and returns the result. The #[wasm_bindgen] attribute tells the compiler that this function should be exposed to JavaScript. Without this, the Rust compiler wouldn't include the function in the generated .wasm module's interface.

Before compiling, open Cargo.toml and confirm that the library section is set to compile as a dynamic C-compatible library (which is required for WebAssembly output):

```
[lib]

crate-type = ["cdylib"]



[dependencies]

wasm-bindgen = "0.2"
```

With your code and configuration in place, it's time to build. Use wasm-pack to compile the Rust source to WebAssembly and generate the JavaScript bindings:

```
wasm-pack build
```

This command will produce output similar to:

```
[INFO]: 🎯   Checking for the Wasm target...
[INFO]: 🌀   Compiling to Wasm...
[INFO]: ⬇️   Installing wasm-bindgen...
[INFO]: ✨   Done in N seconds
[INFO]: 📦    Your wasm pkg is ready to publish at
./pkg.
```

When the command finishes, you'll see a new pkg/ directory. This folder contains everything you need to use your Rust code from JavaScript:

- A `.wasm` binary file with your compiled Rust logic
- A JavaScript glue file that loads and interacts with the Wasm module
- A `package.json` file for npm compatibility
- TypeScript declaration files (if enabled) for auto-completion and type checking

To test that this module works, create a minimal frontend project that loads the `.wasm` file and calls your `square` function from JavaScript. Here's how to do that manually without a bundler:

Create a folder called `demo` and an `index.html` file inside it:

```html
<!-- demo/index.html -->
<!DOCTYPE html>
<html lang="en">
<head>
  <meta charset="UTF-8">
  <title>Rust Wasm Demo</title>
</head>
<body>
  <script type="module">
    import init, { square } from
'../pkg/wasm_math.js';

    async function run() {
      await init();
      console.log(square(6)); // Should print 36
    }

    run();
  </script>
</body>
</html>
```

You can serve this directory using any static HTTP server. For a quick test, install a development server like `serve` using npm:

```
npm install -g serve

serve demo
```

Navigate to `http://localhost:3000` (or whatever port it shows), open the browser console, and you should see `36` printed—indicating that your Rust function was compiled to WebAssembly, loaded in the browser, and executed successfully via JavaScript.

This small example demonstrates the end-to-end pipeline: you write a function in Rust, annotate it for WebAssembly using `#[wasm_bindgen]`, build it with `wasm-pack`, and call it from JavaScript in a real web environment.

Let's extend this with another small exercise. Suppose you want to expose a function that takes a string from JavaScript and returns its length. Here's what that might look like in Rust:

```
#[wasm_bindgen]
pub fn string_length(s: &str) -> usize {
    s.len()
}
```

Rust's `&str` maps cleanly to JavaScript strings, and `usize` corresponds to an integer value. After recompiling with `wasm-pack build`, you can add this function to your frontend code:

```
console.log(string_length("Rust + Wasm")); //
Should print 11
```

By following this method, you now have a repeatable and reliable process for writing Rust functions, compiling them into WebAssembly, and using them in any frontend project—whether you're building with vanilla JavaScript, React, Vue, or another modern framework.

Using `wasm-pack` with npm and Bundlers

Once you've compiled your Rust code into a WebAssembly module using `wasm-pack`, the next step is to bring it into a modern frontend development workflow. Whether you're using React, Vue, or plain JavaScript, `wasm-pack` is designed to make this integration as smooth as possible. It produces an npm-compatible package from your Rust code that includes the compiled `.wasm` binary, JavaScript bindings, and metadata files. With this setup, your WebAssembly module becomes just another module you can `import` in a JavaScript application, alongside your other npm dependencies.

To start, make sure you've already run:

```
wasm-pack build
```

This generates a `pkg/` directory containing everything needed to use your Rust code in a JavaScript project. Inside `pkg/`, you'll find files like `my_module.js`, `my_module_bg.wasm`, `package.json`, and optionally `*.d.ts` TypeScript declarations if enabled.

Now you'll connect this WebAssembly package to a frontend app using npm. Let's walk through a complete example using Vite, which is a fast build tool that works seamlessly with ES Modules and supports modern JavaScript and TypeScript projects.

Create a new frontend project:

```
npm create vite@latest wasm-demo-frontend -- --
template vanilla

cd wasm-demo-frontend

npm install
```

With your frontend project in place, you now need to make your Wasm package accessible to it. If the Rust project is located adjacent to your frontend folder (for example, `../wasm-math/pkg`), you can install it locally using a relative path:

```
npm install ../wasm-math/pkg
```

This registers the package in your `package.json` and allows you to import functions from your Rust-generated `.wasm` module using ES module syntax.

In your `main.js` file (or `main.ts` if you're using TypeScript), you can now import and initialize your Rust-Wasm package like this:

```
import init, { square, string_length } from 'wasm-
math';

init().then(() => {
  console.log(square(8)); // Prints: 64
```

```
    console.log(string_length("Rust + Wasm")); //
Prints: 11
});
```

The `init()` function is automatically generated by `wasm-bindgen` and is required to initialize the Wasm module. It loads the `.wasm` binary asynchronously and prepares all the exported functions for use in JavaScript.

You'll also need to make sure that Vite correctly handles `.wasm` files. Fortunately, Vite supports this out of the box with no additional configuration for most basic use cases. However, if you encounter MIME type errors or issues related to binary file loading, you can explicitly tell Vite to treat `.wasm` files as assets:

```
// vite.config.js
export default {
  assetsInclude: ['**/*.wasm'],
};
```

This ensures that the `.wasm` binary is served correctly during development and bundled properly during production builds.

To see the output in action, run the development server:

npm run dev

Then open your browser to the local server address (usually `http://localhost:5173`). Open the browser console to confirm that the functions from your Rust code are being called correctly and producing the expected output.

Now, let's look at what actually happens when you run `wasm-pack build`. First, it compiles your Rust code to a `.wasm` binary using the `wasm32-unknown-unknown` target. Then it uses `wasm-bindgen` to generate JavaScript glue code that wraps the WebAssembly module and exposes a clean interface. This glue code takes care of translating between JavaScript types and Rust types, especially strings, arrays, and complex objects. Finally, `wasm-pack` creates a `package.json` file that describes your module as an npm package, which can then be used locally or published to the npm registry.

This is particularly powerful because it brings WebAssembly into the same tooling ecosystem developers already use. Whether you're using Vite,

Webpack, or another bundler, the integration works through standard npm and ES module patterns. You don't need to treat your Wasm code as something exotic—just import and use it like any other module.

For larger applications, it's a good practice to modularize your WebAssembly logic and use separate crates for different features. You can publish them to a private npm registry or keep them in your monorepo and install them locally using relative paths. This approach keeps your logic well-organized and lets you share compiled modules across multiple projects.

You can also write TypeScript-friendly WebAssembly modules by enabling TypeScript declaration output when you run `wasm-pack`. To do this, use:

```
wasm-pack build --target bundler --typescript
```

This generates `.d.ts` files alongside your JavaScript wrapper, so you get proper type hints and auto-completion when writing code in editors like VSCode.

wasm-pack bridges the gap between Rust and JavaScript by compiling your code to WebAssembly, generating bindings, and packaging the result in a way that frontend developers are already familiar with. It's what makes Rust + Wasm development practical and productive, not just technically possible. Once this setup is in place, you can continue to write logic in Rust, compile it with `wasm-pack`, and use it directly in your modern frontend workflow.

Chapter 3: Writing Rust for WebAssembly

Writing Rust for WebAssembly is not the same as writing general-purpose Rust. While the language features remain consistent, the **execution environment** for WebAssembly introduces important restrictions that affect what kind of Rust code you can write and how it behaves when compiled to .wasm. In this chapter, we'll unpack those differences and show you how to build effective, idiomatic Rust that runs reliably in a WebAssembly context. You'll also learn how to use key tools like wasm-bindgen, web-sys, and js-sys, and understand how memory and safety are handled when working across language boundaries.

Restrictions of the Wasm Execution Environment

When you compile Rust code to WebAssembly (Wasm), you're targeting an execution environment that is intentionally limited. These constraints exist to ensure performance, portability, and above all, security. But as a developer, understanding these restrictions is crucial because it changes how you approach everything from data access to API usage.

WebAssembly was designed to run in a **sandboxed** environment. In a browser, this means the WebAssembly module is isolated from the underlying operating system. There's no direct access to the file system, no raw sockets, no threads (in most cases), no operating system signals, and no standard system libraries. The execution happens inside a tightly controlled memory space with strict boundaries. This protects the host environment, but it also means that many features you may be used to in native Rust development simply aren't available.

Let's look at one of the most common mistakes new Rust-to-Wasm developers encounter. Suppose you write a function like this:

```rust
use std::fs;

pub fn read_data() -> String {
    fs::read_to_string("data.txt").unwrap()
}
```

This function compiles fine in a native Rust application, but it won't work in WebAssembly when run in the browser. Why? Because `std::fs` depends on file system access, and the Wasm runtime inside the browser doesn't provide it. If you try to compile this for the `wasm32-unknown-unknown` target, you'll get a linker error or runtime panic, depending on how you handle the result.

Instead, you'd have to read the file in JavaScript—say using a `<input type="file">` element—and then pass the content to your WebAssembly module as a string or byte array. WebAssembly has no native concept of files; it relies entirely on the host to provide input.

Here's another example: multithreading. In Rust, it's common to write code that spawns threads to do work in parallel:

```
use std::thread;

pub fn run_threads() {
    thread::spawn(|| {
        println!("Running in another thread!");
    });
}
```

This will not work in WebAssembly (at least not in the default browser setup). WebAssembly itself does not have native thread support in the same way as native platforms. While support for threads using `SharedArrayBuffer` exists behind feature flags and certain browser settings, it's not universally available and comes with significant security considerations.

Because of these constraints, the Rust WebAssembly target (`wasm32-unknown-unknown`) assumes a minimal, freestanding environment. It removes all system-level assumptions, and your code must work without depending on things like file descriptors, TCP sockets, environment variables, or standard input/output.

Even things like `std::time::SystemTime` can behave unexpectedly, since there's no system clock in the WebAssembly execution context. To get the current time, you must call the browser's JavaScript API via Rust bindings—for example, using `js_sys::Date::now()` to get a timestamp in milliseconds.

Let's look at an example that works well in the Wasm environment:

```
use wasm_bindgen::prelude::*;
```

```
use js_sys::Date;

#[wasm_bindgen]
pub fn current_timestamp() -> f64 {
    Date::now()
}
```

This calls JavaScript's `Date.now()` from within Rust and returns a Unix timestamp to JavaScript. It's fast, safe, and fully compatible with the browser environment.

Another key restriction is memory access. In a typical native application, you can allocate and deallocate memory using the heap, and the operating system manages the virtual address space for you. In WebAssembly, you're working with a flat **linear memory** model. This means that memory is represented as a single, contiguous array of bytes. The WebAssembly module is responsible for managing allocations within this space. Tools like `wasm-bindgen` and Rust's allocator handle most of this for you behind the scenes, but you still need to be conscious of memory usage—especially when transferring large data sets between Rust and JavaScript.

For example, passing a large `Vec<u8>` from Rust to JavaScript involves copying that memory from Rust's linear memory into a JavaScript typed array:

```
#[wasm_bindgen]
pub fn get_data() -> Vec<u8> {
    vec![1, 2, 3, 4, 5]
}
```

On the JavaScript side:

```
import init, { get_data } from "your-wasm-module";

await init();
const data = get_data(); // Uint8Array [1, 2, 3, 4,
5]
```

This works well for small data sizes, but if you're dealing with megabytes of image or video data, you'll want to be deliberate about when and how memory is allocated and shared.

Lastly, WebAssembly modules in the browser are not allowed to perform blocking operations. Any kind of blocking call—like a synchronous file read, or a thread sleep—is either unavailable or behaves differently. Instead, asynchronous interaction is the norm. For example, if you want to make a network request from WebAssembly, you must initiate the request through JavaScript (e.g., using `fetch`) and then pass the result back into Rust.

Here's a conceptual flow:

1. JavaScript performs the `fetch()` call.
2. When the response is received, the body is read as text or binary.
3. The result is passed into a Rust function exported from your Wasm module.

This pattern can feel awkward at first, but it's necessary because Wasm modules don't have access to JavaScript's event loop or browser APIs directly—they must be mediated through bindings.

The WebAssembly environment imposes strict limits on system access, threading, and synchronous I/O. But these restrictions are part of what makes it fast, secure, and portable. When writing Rust code for Wasm, your goal is to focus on the core logic—computation, data transformation, memory safety—while relying on JavaScript to interact with the outside world. By understanding and respecting these boundaries, you'll write code that works reliably across browsers, loads quickly, and behaves consistently for all users.

Working Within `no_std` Limitations

When compiling Rust code to WebAssembly for the browser using the `wasm32-unknown-unknown` target, you're working in an environment where much of the standard Rust library is not available. This is because the target platform—WebAssembly—does not provide the operating system and system-level services that the full `std` library depends on. As a result, whether you explicitly write `#![no_std]` or not, your code must conform to the same restrictions that apply in `no_std` environments. Understanding what this means in practice is essential if you're going to build reliable, portable, and performant Rust-Wasm applications.

In a `no_std` environment, you don't get access to `std`. But with the right support, you still have `core` and often `alloc`. This is exactly the case when building WebAssembly with Rust: you can use heap-allocated data structures, but you cannot rely on anything that expects an operating system.

Let's look at an example. You can write this just fine in WebAssembly:

```
#[wasm_bindgen]
pub fn repeat_string(s: &str, times: usize) ->
String {
    s.repeat(times)
}
```

Even though `String` and `str` involve heap allocations, this compiles and runs because the `wasm-bindgen` toolchain sets up a global allocator for you. This allocator uses the Wasm module's linear memory for dynamic memory operations. You don't need to worry about managing that memory manually, but it's good to know that everything is happening within a single flat address space defined by the WebAssembly runtime.

On the other hand, you cannot do something like this:

```
use std::fs;

#[wasm_bindgen]
pub fn read_file() -> String {
    fs::read_to_string("data.txt").unwrap()
}
```

This will fail because the file system APIs are part of `std`, and there's no file system accessible in the WebAssembly execution environment (in browsers). Even if you used `wasm32-wasi` (WebAssembly System Interface) for server-side applications, it wouldn't help in the browser, where such APIs are simply unavailable.

What about threads? Multithreading in Rust relies on `std::thread`, which again is not available in the browser environment. While WebAssembly has started to support threads through `SharedArrayBuffer` and atomics, these features are not universally supported and must be enabled with caution. By default, threading is not available, and Rust's concurrency features like `std::thread::spawn()` cannot be used.

Instead, concurrency is achieved using JavaScript promises and Rust async functions—though these too must be mediated by JavaScript, since

WebAssembly doesn't have an async execution model built-in. If you want to perform asynchronous tasks in a WebAssembly module, you often write the async logic in JavaScript and pass results into Rust via function arguments or callbacks.

Here's a small but practical example that works within no_std limitations. It performs a simple text transformation:

```
#[wasm_bindgen]
pub fn reverse(input: &str) -> String {
    input.chars().rev().collect()
}
```

This is fully compliant with the constraints of the WebAssembly target. It uses chars() to iterate over Unicode scalar values, reverses the iterator, and collects them back into a String. All of this is done using types from core and alloc, so it works without requiring access to the system or standard I/O.

If you want to build larger applications, such as interactive tools or data processors, the key is to separate concerns. Keep your Rust-Wasm code focused on **pure computation**—anything that can be done without relying on OS-level functionality—and delegate all I/O, DOM manipulation, networking, and asynchronous behavior to JavaScript.

For example, suppose you're building an image filter. Your Rust code should accept a byte array representing raw pixel data, process it, and return the result. JavaScript would handle loading the image from the filesystem, converting it to a buffer, and drawing the filtered image on a canvas.

Here's a conceptual Rust function for modifying pixel brightness:

```
#[wasm_bindgen]
pub fn adjust_brightness(data: &mut [u8], amount:
i16) {
    for byte in data.iter_mut() {
        let value = *byte as i16 + amount;
        *byte = value.clamp(0, 255) as u8;
    }
}
```

This works entirely within no_std boundaries. The function takes a mutable slice of bytes, modifies it in-place, and requires no I/O or OS-level dependencies. JavaScript is responsible for preparing and handling the data before and after the call.

Working within `no_std` limitations when targeting WebAssembly means writing Rust code that is self-contained, portable, and independent of system services. You can use most core data types and dynamic memory, thanks to the `alloc` crate and WebAssembly's linear memory. But you must avoid features from `std` that require a full OS, such as file I/O, threading, and process management. By respecting these boundaries and offloading external interactions to JavaScript, you can build powerful and efficient WebAssembly modules with Rust that integrate cleanly into web applications.

Understanding **wasm-bindgen**, **web-sys**, and **js-sys**

When working with Rust and WebAssembly in the browser, one of the key challenges is enabling **communication between your Rust code and the JavaScript environment**. WebAssembly itself doesn't come with built-in access to browser APIs like `document`, `window`, `console`, or `fetch`. Instead, these APIs are only accessible through JavaScript, which acts as the host environment. To make your Rust code talk to JavaScript—and vice versa— you need a bridge that can translate types, expose functions, and manage memory across the language boundary. This is where `wasm-bindgen`, `web-sys`, and `js-sys` come into play.

`wasm-bindgen`: Bridging Rust and JavaScript

`wasm-bindgen` is the most critical tool in the Rust WebAssembly toolchain. It provides the glue code that connects your compiled Rust code to JavaScript. This includes:

- Exposing Rust functions and types to JavaScript
- Allowing you to call JavaScript functions from Rust
- Handling type conversion between the two languages
- Managing memory allocation and deallocation safely

When you mark a Rust function with the `#[wasm_bindgen]` attribute, you're telling the compiler to make that function available to JavaScript. Here's a simple example:

```
use wasm_bindgen::prelude::*;

#[wasm_bindgen]
pub fn greet(name: &str) -> String {
    format!("Hello, {}!", name)
}
```

After you build this with `wasm-pack`, it generates both a `.wasm` binary and a JavaScript wrapper that allows you to call this function like any other JavaScript function:

```
import init, { greet } from 'my-wasm-lib';

await init();
console.log(greet("Rust")); // Output: Hello, Rust!
```

`wasm-bindgen` takes care of converting the JavaScript string into a format that Rust can work with (`&str`), and it converts the Rust `String` into a JavaScript string automatically. Without `wasm-bindgen`, you would need to manually manage memory, handle raw pointers, and deal with encoding formats between UTF-8 and UTF-16—an error-prone and time-consuming process.

It also supports more complex types like structs, enums, `Vec<T>`, and optional values. For example:

```
#[wasm_bindgen]
pub fn sum(numbers: Vec<i32>) -> i32 {
    numbers.iter().sum()
}
```

You can pass a JavaScript array to this function, and `wasm-bindgen` will convert it into a `Vec<i32>` for you behind the scenes.

js-sys: Accessing JavaScript Built-ins

While `wasm-bindgen` helps you bind functions and types between Rust and JavaScript, sometimes you need access to built-in JavaScript objects—things like `Math`, `Date`, or `Promise`. That's where the `js-sys` crate comes in. It provides safe, idiomatic Rust bindings for JavaScript's core standard objects.

Let's say you want to generate a timestamp in Rust using JavaScript's
`Date.now()`:

```
use wasm_bindgen::prelude::*;
use js_sys::Date;

#[wasm_bindgen]
pub fn now() -> f64 {
    Date::now()
}
```

This gives you access to the exact same API you would use in JavaScript, but
from within Rust. The value returned is a `f64` (floating point), which
represents the number of milliseconds since the Unix epoch.

Another example: using JavaScript's `Math.random()` in Rust:

```
use js_sys::Math;

#[wasm_bindgen]
pub fn random_value() -> f64 {
    Math::random()
}
```

Under the hood, this is calling into the browser's native `Math` object. `js-sys`
is especially useful when you want to use common JavaScript built-ins without
writing a separate JavaScript function or dealing with manual bindings.

web sys: - Working with Browser APIs

While `js-sys` gives you access to standard JavaScript objects, `web-sys` is a
much larger crate that provides bindings for **the full Web API surface—**
everything defined by the Web IDL specification. This includes the DOM,
HTML elements, canvas, events, WebSockets, fetch, and much more.

Here's an example of writing a message to the JavaScript console from Rust:

```
use web_sys::console;

#[wasm_bindgen]
pub fn log_message() {
```

```
    console::log_1(&"This is Rust logging to the
browser console!".into());
}
```

This is equivalent to calling `console.log("...")` in JavaScript. `console::log_1` is a typed function that accepts a single `&JsValue`, which is the basic representation of a JavaScript value in Rust.

Suppose you want to interact with the DOM—for example, set the text of an HTML element with a specific ID. You can do it like this:

```
use wasm_bindgen::prelude::*;
use web_sys::{window, Document};

#[wasm_bindgen]
pub fn update_text(id: &str, text: &str) {
    let window = window().expect("should have a
Window");
    let document = window.document().expect("should
have a Document");

    if let Some(element) =
document.get_element_by_id(id) {
        element.set_inner_html(text);
    }
}
```

This function locates an element by its ID and updates its inner HTML. It uses `web_sys::window()` to get access to the global window object, then uses the document to find and manipulate DOM elements—all from within Rust.

You can also respond to user input, interact with the canvas, and call APIs like `fetch`, `requestAnimationFrame`, or `AudioContext`—everything you'd normally do in JavaScript.

Putting It All Together

Let's build a more complete example: a Rust function that logs the current time to the console using JavaScript APIs, all accessed through `js-sys` and `web-sys`.

```
use wasm_bindgen::prelude::*;
```

```
use js_sys::Date;
use web_sys::console;

#[wasm_bindgen]
pub fn log_time() {
    let now = Date::new_0();
    let time_string =
now.to_locale_time_string("en-US");
    console::log_1(&time_string.into());
}
```

This function creates a `Date` object in Rust using `js-sys`, formats it using JavaScript's `toLocaleTimeString`, and sends it to the browser console using `web-sys`.

All of this runs safely and efficiently because `wasm-bindgen` manages the boundaries, `js-sys` exposes native JavaScript objects, and `web-sys` handles browser-specific APIs.

If you're writing Rust for the Web, understanding how to work with `wasm-bindgen`, `js-sys`, and `web-sys` is essential. These tools allow you to:

- Expose Rust functions and types to JavaScript
- Call JavaScript functions and manipulate browser APIs from Rust
- Safely and efficiently convert types across the Wasm boundary

They are not just utilities—they are the foundation of all meaningful WebAssembly interop in the browser. With them, you can write clean, safe, performant Rust code that works side-by-side with modern web technologies. In the next section, you'll learn how memory is managed across the boundary and how Rust preserves safety even when working with JavaScript objects.

Memory Safety and Cross-Language Interop

One of the most powerful advantages Rust brings to WebAssembly development is **guaranteed memory safety without requiring a garbage collector**. This is a big deal, especially when your code needs to interoperate across the boundary between Rust and JavaScript. On one side, you have Rust's strict compile-time ownership model, which ensures that memory cannot be accessed after it's freed, cannot be simultaneously modified from multiple places without synchronization, and cannot be null unless explicitly allowed. On the other side, you have JavaScript, a dynamically typed, garbage-collected language where memory is managed by a runtime engine that you don't control.

When these two models meet—Rust's static memory discipline and JavaScript's dynamic memory allocation—you need a system that translates between them safely and efficiently. That's where `wasm-bindgen`, **linear memory**, and **typed views** come in.

Understanding Linear Memory in Wasm

WebAssembly defines a **flat, contiguous block of memory** called *linear memory*. This memory is accessible both from within the compiled WebAssembly module and, when exported, from JavaScript as an `ArrayBuffer`. When you compile Rust to Wasm, the Rust allocator (provided by `wee_alloc` or the default `dlmalloc`) uses this linear memory space to manage heap allocations like `String`, `Vec`, and `Box`.

All dynamic data lives inside this memory block. Rust knows exactly how this memory is structured, and `wasm-bindgen` helps safely expose or receive data across the language boundary.

If you write the following Rust function:

```
#[wasm_bindgen]
pub fn make_buffer() -> Vec<u8> {
    vec![1, 2, 3, 4, 5]
}
```

and compile it with `wasm-pack`, you can call it from JavaScript like this:

```
import init, { make_buffer } from
"./my_wasm_module/pkg/my_wasm_module.js";

await init();
const data = make_buffer(); // this is a Uint8Array
```

The Rust `Vec<u8>` is automatically translated into a JavaScript `Uint8Array` using the glue code generated by `wasm-bindgen`. You don't need to copy the memory manually or worry about alignment—it's handled for you. This translation happens efficiently by referencing the underlying linear memory directly through a view.

Now let's look at the reverse case: passing data from JavaScript into Rust.

Passing Data Into Rust

Suppose you want to write a function that receives binary data from JavaScript:

```
#[wasm_bindgen]
pub fn sum_bytes(data: &[u8]) -> u32 {
    data.iter().map(|&b| b as u32).sum()
}
```

From JavaScript, you can pass a `Uint8Array`:

```
const bytes = new Uint8Array([10, 20, 30, 40]);

const total = sum_bytes(bytes); // should return 100
```

Under the hood, `wasm-bindgen` copies the data into Rust's linear memory and hands over a safe reference to it. In this case, the `&[u8]` slice is constructed from the `Uint8Array` passed in. The data is immutable here, but you can also pass a `&mut [u8]` from JavaScript to Rust if you want Rust to modify it in-place—useful for audio buffers, image data, or shared memory processing.

Here's a slightly more advanced example. Let's say you want to implement a filter that normalizes pixel values in an image:

```
#[wasm_bindgen]
pub fn normalize(data: &mut [u8]) {
    let max = *data.iter().max().unwrap_or(&1) as f32;
    for pixel in data.iter_mut() {
        *pixel = ((*pixel as f32) / max * 255.0) as u8;
    }
}
```

On the JavaScript side:

```
const imgData = new Uint8Array([30, 60, 90, 120]);
normalize(imgData);
```

```
// imgData is now normalized so the highest value
is 255
```

In this case, memory is being shared temporarily with Rust and modified directly. You still get memory safety because the mutation is scoped within the function, and Rust's borrow checker ensures that no other references to the same data are used unsafely during that time.

Managing Strings Across the Boundary

Strings are more complex than byte arrays because JavaScript uses UTF-16 encoded strings and Rust uses UTF-8. To bridge the gap, wasm-bindgen automatically handles the conversion when you use &str or String in Rust function signatures.

Here's a basic function:

```
#[wasm_bindgen]

pub fn welcome(name: &str) -> String {

    format!("Welcome, {}!", name)

}
```

This can be called from JavaScript like this:

```
const message = welcome("Ada");

console.log(message); // "Welcome, Ada!"
```

In this example, wasm-bindgen converts the JS string ("Ada") into a UTF-8 byte array, passes it to Rust, and then converts the resulting Rust String back into a JS string before returning it. This process involves copying the string data into linear memory on one side and decoding it on the other—but it's safe and reliable.

However, if you're calling this function in a loop with large or frequently changing strings, you should be aware of the cost of these conversions. In performance-sensitive applications, consider reusing buffers or passing numeric handles instead of full strings when possible.

Ownership and Lifetime Across Boundaries

Rust's strict ownership model does not apply in JavaScript. JavaScript doesn't know (or care) about lifetimes, borrowing, or ownership rules. That means it's your responsibility, when crossing the boundary, to make sure memory doesn't get used after it's freed.

For example, if you pass a pointer from Rust to JavaScript—say using raw memory for manual interop—you need to be absolutely sure that you don't free the memory in Rust while JavaScript is still using it. This is rare when using `wasm-bindgen`, but if you're writing low-level bindings or trying to share memory manually, it's something to watch for.

In most typical usage, though, `wasm-bindgen` ensures safe interop by **retaining ownership of memory inside Rust** and only exposing read/write access through typed wrappers.

For more advanced use cases—like sharing memory buffers between threads (where supported), or reusing pre-allocated Wasm memory—you can use WebAssembly's `memory` export and manage memory allocation manually. But that comes with its own complexity and is not required in most applications.

Debugging Memory Issues

If you suspect a memory issue, tools like Chrome's WebAssembly Memory Inspector can help. You can visualize the Wasm memory buffer, view live allocations, and step through JavaScript-Wasm interop to ensure your data is moving correctly.

In Rust, you can also use `console_log` or `web_sys::console::log_1()` to inspect the content of arrays, lengths, and pointer addresses when debugging:

```
use web_sys::console;

#[wasm_bindgen]
pub fn log_first_byte(data: &[u8]) {
    if let Some(&first) = data.first() {
        console::log_1(&format!("First byte: {}",
first).into());
    }
}
```

This technique allows you to verify the correctness of values at the Wasm boundary and debug potential off-by-one or memory corruption issues.

Rust's memory model is a perfect match for WebAssembly's linear memory architecture, and `wasm-bindgen` makes cross-language interoperability both safe and ergonomic. Whether you're passing numbers, strings, or byte arrays, the conversions are handled transparently and efficiently. When you need low-level control, it's available—but most of the time, you'll benefit from Rust's safety guarantees without needing to manage memory manually.

Understanding how memory flows between Rust and JavaScript—and how ownership and lifetimes work in this context—is the key to writing high-performance, safe WebAssembly applications that interact confidently with the web platform.

Chapter 4: Calling JavaScript from Rust and Vice Versa

Integrating Rust with WebAssembly isn't just about compiling safe, fast code that runs in the browser—it's also about making that code interact meaningfully with the **JavaScript environment**. The real power of this toolchain comes from the fact that Rust and JavaScript can **call each other**, pass data back and forth, and build seamless applications together.

In this chapter, you'll learn how to bridge Rust and JavaScript, convert values between their type systems, respond to browser events using callbacks, and pass more complex data like arrays and structured objects across the Wasm boundary.

Bridging Rust and JavaScript

When you're working with WebAssembly in the browser, it's important to understand that **JavaScript is the host**, and **WebAssembly is the guest**. Your Rust code compiled to WebAssembly can't do anything on its own—it can't access the DOM, can't fetch data from the network, and can't handle input without JavaScript facilitating it.

To bridge this gap, Rust provides the `wasm-bindgen` crate. This tool allows you to:

- **Call JavaScript functions from Rust**
- **Expose Rust functions to be called from JavaScript**
- **Convert types across the boundary safely**

Let's start by exposing a simple Rust function that JavaScript can call:

```rust
use wasm_bindgen::prelude::*;

#[wasm_bindgen]
pub fn greet(name: &str) -> String {
    format!("Hello, {}!", name)
}
```

After compiling this with `wasm-pack build`, JavaScript can import and use this function:

```
import init, { greet } from
'./pkg/your_module_name.js';

await init();
console.log(greet("Ada")); // Output: Hello, Ada!
```

This direction—from Rust to JavaScript—is the most common one when you're building modules that implement logic or computation. But you can also go the other way: **invoke JavaScript functions directly from within Rust**.

Working with `JsValue` and Type Conversions

To interact with JavaScript from Rust, you need a type that can represent anything JavaScript can produce—numbers, strings, objects, arrays, functions, and even `undefined`. In the `wasm-bindgen` ecosystem, this universal type is called `JsValue`.

You use `JsValue` to pass data in and out of JavaScript, either explicitly or via conversions provided by `wasm-bindgen`.

Here's how to call a JavaScript function from Rust using `JsValue` and the `js_sys` crate:

```
use wasm_bindgen::prelude::*;
use js_sys::Math;

#[wasm_bindgen]
pub fn random_between(min: f64, max: f64) -> f64 {
    let value = Math::random(); // JS:
Math.random()
    min + (value * (max - min))
}
```

Here, you're calling the JavaScript `Math.random()` function from Rust, wrapping the value in a `f64`, and returning the result.

But sometimes, you need to work directly with values coming from or going into JavaScript in a generic way. For instance, you may want to log a raw JavaScript value in the console:

```
use wasm_bindgen::JsValue;
use web_sys::console;

#[wasm_bindgen]
pub fn log_value(value: JsValue) {
    console::log_1(&value);
}
```

You can then call this from JavaScript:

```
log_value("Logging from JS");

log_value({ x: 42, y: 13 });
```

Rust doesn't know the structure of the JavaScript object, but it can receive it, hold it, or pass it around as a JsValue. If you need to extract fields, you can cast it using js_sys::Object, or use serde-wasm-bindgen for more structured data.

Handling Events and Callbacks

If you're building any sort of interactive application, you need to respond to **events**—clicks, key presses, animation frames, and more. In traditional JavaScript, this is straightforward, but in Rust, it requires setting up a **callback** that can be passed to JavaScript and invoked when needed.

Here's how to set up a Rust function that listens to a button click:

```
use wasm_bindgen::prelude::*;
use wasm_bindgen::closure::Closure;
use web_sys::{window, Document, HtmlElement};

#[wasm_bindgen(start)]
pub fn start() -> Result<(), JsValue> {
    let document: Document =
window().unwrap().document().unwrap();
    let button = document.get_element_by_id("my-
button").unwrap();
```

44

```rust
    let closure = Closure::wrap(Box::new(move || {
        web_sys::console::log_1(&"Button
clicked!".into());
    }) as Box<dyn Fn()>);

    button
        .dyn_ref::<HtmlElement>()
        .unwrap()

.set_onclick(Some(closure.as_ref().unchecked_ref())
);

    closure.forget(); // Prevent memory from being
deallocated
    Ok(())
}
```

Let's break this down:

- You create a `Closure` wrapping a Rust function.
- You cast the function to `Box<dyn Fn()>` so it can be passed to JavaScript.
- You attach it as an `onclick` event handler to a DOM element.
- You call `.forget()` to tell Rust not to clean up the closure, because JavaScript will keep using it.

This pattern allows you to respond to DOM events directly from Rust with full memory safety.

Passing Complex Data Structures Across the Boundary

For more advanced use cases, you may need to pass structured data—like objects or arrays of objects—between JavaScript and Rust. In these cases, you can use either raw `JsValue` representations or the powerful serialization capabilities of the `serde` ecosystem.

Let's say you want to accept a JSON object from JavaScript and work with it as a native Rust struct. First, define your data model:

```rust
use wasm_bindgen::prelude::*;
use serde::{Deserialize, Serialize};
```

```rust
#[derive(Deserialize)]
pub struct Point {
    x: f64,
    y: f64,
}

#[wasm_bindgen]
pub fn process_point(point: JsValue) -> f64 {
    let point: Point = point.into_serde().unwrap();
    (point.x.powi(2) + point.y.powi(2)).sqrt()
}
```

From JavaScript:

```javascript
process_point({ x: 3, y: 4 }); // returns 5
```

In this example, you're leveraging `serde` and `serde-wasm-bindgen` (which you must include in your `Cargo.toml`) to deserialize JavaScript objects into Rust structs. This enables type-safe interop without manually unpacking fields.

Similarly, you can return structured data from Rust to JavaScript:

```rust
#[derive(Serialize)]
pub struct Person {
    name: String,
    age: u32,
}

#[wasm_bindgen]
pub fn get_person() -> JsValue {
    let person = Person {
        name: "Ada".to_string(),
        age: 32,
    };
    JsValue::from_serde(&person).unwrap()
}
```

From JavaScript:

```javascript
const person = get_person();
```

```
console.log(person.name); // "Ada"

console.log(person.age);  // 32
```

This pattern makes it much easier to exchange meaningful data between both languages while maintaining correctness and structure.

Rust and JavaScript are fundamentally different in how they manage memory, type safety, and execution, but with the right tools—especially wasm-bindgen and its supporting crates—you can build clean, powerful bridges between them.

Bridging Rust and JavaScript

When you're building WebAssembly applications with Rust, your code doesn't operate in isolation. It runs inside an environment that is entirely controlled by JavaScript. That means if you want to display anything on the screen, respond to user input, fetch data, or interact with the browser in any meaningful way, you need to **connect your Rust logic to JavaScript**. This connection—calling functions, sharing data, and handling behavior across the two languages—is what we refer to as **bridging Rust and JavaScript**.

Rust and JavaScript speak very different languages under the hood. Rust is compiled, strictly typed, and enforces ownership and memory safety. JavaScript is interpreted (or JIT-compiled), dynamically typed, and garbage-collected. Bridging the two requires a tool that understands both sides. In the Rust WebAssembly ecosystem, that tool is wasm-bindgen.

Exporting Rust Functions to JavaScript

The most common use case is exposing Rust functions to be called from JavaScript. You might write a high-performance algorithm in Rust, then call it from your frontend code to improve performance.

Let's write a simple example: a function that calculates the factorial of a number.

```
use wasm_bindgen::prelude::*;

#[wasm_bindgen]
pub fn factorial(n: u32) -> u64 {
```

```
    (1..=n).map(|x| x as u64).product()
}
```

This function is marked with the `#[wasm_bindgen]` attribute. This tells the compiler and `wasm-bindgen` to generate the glue code that allows JavaScript to call it.

After running `wasm-pack build`, you'll get a `pkg/` directory containing JavaScript and WebAssembly files. Now, from your frontend:

```
import init, { factorial } from
'./pkg/your_wasm_module.js';

await init(); // must call this before using the
module
console.log(factorial(10)); // prints 3628800
```

That's it. You've called native-compiled Rust code from JavaScript.

Importing JavaScript Functions into Rust

You can also go the other direction: call JavaScript from within your Rust code. This is useful when you need access to browser APIs like `alert`, `console.log`, `Date.now()`, or custom JavaScript functions you've written.

Here's how to call the built-in `alert()` function:

```
use wasm_bindgen::prelude::*;

#[wasm_bindgen]
extern "C" {
    pub fn alert(s: &str);
}

#[wasm_bindgen]
pub fn notify_user(name: &str) {
    let message = format!("Welcome, {}!", name);
    alert(&message);
}
```

In this code:

- The `extern "C"` block declares the JavaScript function signature.
- The `alert()` function becomes available in Rust just like any other Rust function.
- You can now call `notify_user("Grace")` from JavaScript and trigger an alert box from within Rust.

This type of binding is useful for accessing any JavaScript global or third-party libraries.

Bridging Custom JavaScript Functions

You're not limited to calling built-in browser APIs. You can also define your own JavaScript functions and call them from Rust.

Suppose you have this JavaScript function:

```
export function square(x) {
    return x * x;
}
```

You can bind to it in Rust like this:

```
#[wasm_bindgen]
extern "C" {
    pub fn square(x: i32) -> i32;
}

#[wasm_bindgen]
pub fn use_square(n: i32) -> i32 {
    square(n) + 10
}
```

If you call `use_square(4)` from JavaScript, it calls your JS `square()` function from within Rust, adds 10, and returns `26`.

This gives you a lot of flexibility. You can implement UI logic or DOM interactions in JavaScript while keeping the compute-heavy parts in Rust.

Sharing JavaScript Objects and State

Sometimes, you want to pass a JavaScript object to Rust, do something with it, and possibly return a result. You can do this using `JsValue`.

Let's say you want to call `console.log()` from Rust:

```rust
use wasm_bindgen::prelude::*;
use web_sys::console;

#[wasm_bindgen]
pub fn log_message(message: &str) {
    console::log_1(&JsValue::from_str(message));
}
```

You can now write:

```rust
log_message("This message was logged from Rust!");
```

Rust does not natively support dynamic types, so `JsValue` is used as a universal wrapper for anything that comes from or goes to JavaScript. It represents strings, numbers, arrays, objects, booleans, and more.

Practical Example: Compute in Rust, Render in JS

Let's go through a real-world case. Suppose you're building a tool that generates a SHA-256 hash of a string. You want the hash calculation to happen in Rust for performance and safety, but the UI will be handled in JavaScript.

In Rust (`lib.rs`):

```rust
use wasm_bindgen::prelude::*;
use sha2::{Sha256, Digest};

#[wasm_bindgen]
pub fn hash_string(input: &str) -> String {
    let mut hasher = Sha256::new();
    hasher.update(input);
    let result = hasher.finalize();
    format!("{:x}", result)
}
```

You'd build this with `wasm-pack`, then use it in JavaScript:

```
import init, { hash_string } from "./pkg/hasher";

await init();

document.querySelector("#hash-
button").addEventListener("click", () => {
  const input =
document.querySelector("#input").value;
  const output = hash_string(input);
  document.querySelector("#output").textContent =
output;
});
```

Now you've successfully built a frontend where UI and interactivity are managed in JavaScript, but performance-critical hashing logic is handled in Rust. This is a strong example of bridging languages for practical benefit.

The key to building productive Rust and WebAssembly applications is mastering the interface between Rust and JavaScript. Whether you're exporting functions from Rust, calling JavaScript APIs from Rust, sharing objects, or wrapping values in `JsValue`, the `wasm-bindgen` ecosystem gives you the tools to make this communication clean, safe, and efficient.

Working with `JsValue` and Type Conversions

When writing WebAssembly applications with Rust that interact with JavaScript, one of the most fundamental challenges you'll face is handling **data** between the two languages. Rust is statically typed and designed to know exactly what kind of data it's working with at compile time. JavaScript, by contrast, is dynamic—it can pass anything to a function at runtime without declaring types up front.

To bridge this gap, Rust uses a special type: `JsValue`. Provided by the `wasm-bindgen` crate, `JsValue` is a flexible wrapper that can represent **any JavaScript value**: numbers, strings, booleans, arrays, objects, `null`, `undefined`, or even functions. It is the universal building block for **cross-language communication** when the types don't match exactly—or when you need to accept or return something that varies in shape.

Accepting JavaScript Values in Rust Using `JsValue`

Let's say you're building a Rust function that needs to accept a dynamic value—something that might be a string, a number, or an object. Instead of committing to one specific type in Rust, you can accept a `JsValue`.

```
use wasm_bindgen::prelude::*;
use wasm_bindgen::JsValue;
use web_sys::console;

#[wasm_bindgen]
pub fn print_js_value(val: JsValue) {
    console::log_1(&val);
}
```

Now in JavaScript, you can call this with anything:

```
print_js_value("hello");              // logs:
hello
print_js_value(42);                   // logs: 42
print_js_value({ name: "Rust" });     // logs:
[object Object]
print_js_value(null);                 // logs: null
```

Rust doesn't attempt to interpret the value unless you explicitly tell it to. `console::log_1()` prints the raw `JsValue`, letting JavaScript handle formatting.

This is useful for logging, diagnostics, and receiving flexible input from the web.

Extracting Data from `JsValue` in Rust

If you want to work with the actual content of a `JsValue`, you need to **convert it into a concrete Rust type**. This is done with the `.as_` methods for primitives, or by deserializing using serde wasm bindgen for structured data.

Let's extract a number from a `JsValue`:

```
#[wasm_bindgen]
pub fn double_if_number(val: JsValue) -> JsValue {
    if let Some(n) = val.as_f64() {
        JsValue::from_f64(n * 2.0)
```

```
    } else {
        JsValue::from_str("Not a number")
    }
}
```

From JavaScript:

```
console.log(double_if_number(10));    // 20

console.log(double_if_number("hi")); // "Not a
number"
```

This technique gives you a way to safely inspect and manipulate values passed from JavaScript, handling cases where the types don't match what you expect.

You can also extract strings:

```
#[wasm_bindgen]
pub fn greet_if_string(val: JsValue) -> JsValue {
    if let Some(s) = val.as_string() {
        JsValue::from_str(&format!("Hello, {}!",
s))
    } else {
        JsValue::from_str("Expected a string")
    }
}
```

And booleans:

```
#[wasm_bindgen]
pub fn invert(val: JsValue) -> JsValue {
    if let Some(b) = val.as_bool() {
        JsValue::from_bool(!b)
    } else {
        JsValue::from_str("Not a boolean")
    }
}
```

Deserializing JavaScript Objects into Rust Structs

If you want to handle structured data—like objects or arrays—use the serde_wasm_bindgen crate. It provides safe, type-aware conversions between JsValue and Rust's serde-compatible types.

First, add the dependencies in Cargo.toml:

```toml
[dependencies]

wasm-bindgen = "0.2"

serde = { version = "1.0", features = ["derive"] }

serde_wasm_bindgen = "0.5"
```

Now suppose you're passed an object like { x: 4, y: 3 }. You can define a struct:

```rust
use serde::Deserialize;
use serde_wasm_bindgen;
use wasm_bindgen::prelude::*;

#[derive(Deserialize)]
pub struct Point {
    x: i32,
    y: i32,
}

#[wasm_bindgen]
pub fn magnitude(val: JsValue) -> Result<f64,
JsValue> {
    let point: Point =
serde_wasm_bindgen::from_value(val)?;
    let length = ((point.x.pow(2) + point.y.pow(2))
as f64).sqrt();
    Ok(length)
}
```

JavaScript:

```javascript
console.log(magnitude({ x: 3, y: 4 })); // 5
```

The Rust function uses `serde_wasm_bindgen::from_value()` to deserialize the object. If the structure doesn't match, it returns a `JsValue` error, which you can catch or log in JavaScript.

You can also do the reverse: return a structured Rust type to JavaScript.

```
use serde::Serialize;

#[derive(Serialize)]
pub struct User {
    username: String,
    age: u32,
}

#[wasm_bindgen]
pub fn get_user() -> JsValue {
    let user = User {
        username: "rustacean".into(),
        age: 28,
    };
    serde_wasm_bindgen::to_value(&user).unwrap()
}
```

JavaScript:

```
const user = get_user();

console.log(user.username); // "rustacean"

console.log(user.age);       // 28
```

Converting Rust Types to JavaScript

The reverse of all this—converting Rust types into JavaScript-friendly `JsValue`s—is handled using `JsValue::from_*()` functions.

- `JsValue::from_str("hi")`
- `JsValue::from_f64(3.14)`
- `JsValue::from_bool(true)`
- `JsValue::from_serde(&my_struct).unwrap()`

These conversions are automatic when you return values from Rust functions annotated with #[wasm_bindgen]. For example, returning a String or a bool from a #[wasm_bindgen] function automatically produces a JS string or boolean.

Handling Arrays and Typed Data

You can also work directly with arrays. Rust slices and Vecs of numbers can be exposed to JavaScript as typed arrays.

```
#[wasm_bindgen]
pub fn make_array() -> Vec<i32> {
    vec![1, 2, 3, 4, 5]
}
```

JavaScript:

```
const arr = make_array(); // Int32Array

console.log(arr[2]); // 3
```

For custom logic, you can use js_sys::Array and js_sys::Object to construct and inspect JS structures directly from Rust.

When you're working across the Rust-JavaScript boundary, JsValue is your foundation. It's how you accept dynamic input from JavaScript and how you return results back. While you lose some of Rust's strict type checking at the interface, you can restore it using pattern matching, conversion helpers, or full-blown serde deserialization for structured objects.

Mastering JsValue gives you precise control over how Rust interacts with the JavaScript world—and unlocks the full potential of using Rust in a WebAssembly context. Whether you're building a plugin for a frontend app, a graphics filter, or a secure parser, working fluently with values between languages is a skill you'll use in every project.

Handling Events and Callbacks

When building WebAssembly applications that interact with web pages, your Rust code often needs to **respond to user actions**—like button clicks, input changes, or keyboard presses. In JavaScript, these interactions are typically handled with event listeners and callbacks. In Rust, you can achieve the same result using `Closure` objects from `wasm-bindgen`, combined with browser APIs from `web-sys`.

However, because Rust doesn't have a garbage collector or dynamic dispatch like JavaScript, event handling must be approached with a clear understanding of ownership, lifetime, and memory management.

The Challenge: Passing a Function from Rust to JavaScript

When JavaScript attaches an event listener, it passes a callback function like this:

```
document.getElementById("btn").addEventListener("click", () => {
    console.log("Clicked!");
});
```

To achieve the same from Rust, you need to:

1. Define a Rust function or closure that implements `Fn` or `FnMut`.
2. Wrap that closure using `wasm_bindgen::closure::Closure`.
3. Pass a reference to that closure to a DOM method using `web-sys`.
4. Manage the memory so the closure lives as long as the DOM needs it.

Let's start with a basic example.

Example: Button Click Event Handler

This example logs a message when a button is clicked. First, ensure the HTML includes:

```
<button id="click-me">Click Me</button>
```

Now in Rust:

```
use wasm_bindgen::prelude::*;
use wasm_bindgen::JsCast;
use web_sys::{window, Document, HtmlElement};

#[wasm_bindgen(start)]
```

```rust
pub fn start() -> Result<(), JsValue> {
    let window = window().ok_or("no global `window`
exists")?;
    let document = window.document().ok_or("should
have a document")?;
    let button = document
        .get_element_by_id("click-me")
        .ok_or("no element with id 'click-me'")?;

    let button = button.dyn_into::<HtmlElement>()?;

    let closure = Closure::wrap(Box::new(move || {
        web_sys::console::log_1(&"Button was
clicked!".into());
    }) as Box<dyn Fn()>);


button.set_onclick(Some(closure.as_ref().unchecked_
ref()));

    closure.forget(); // Important: keep closure
alive
    Ok(())
}
```

Here's what's happening step-by-step:

- We get a reference to the document and then to the button element by ID.
- We cast the element to HtmlElement so that we can call set_onclick.
- We define a Rust closure wrapped in a Closure type, which implements wasm-bindgen's callable traits.
- We pass the reference using .as_ref().unchecked_ref()—this is a safe cast from a typed Rust closure to a JavaScript-compatible function pointer.
- Finally, we call .forget() to intentionally **leak** the memory for the closure. This is necessary because otherwise, the closure would be dropped and deallocated at the end of the function, making the JavaScript reference invalid.

In practice, `.forget()` is used for event listeners that last the entire life of the page. If you plan to remove them later, you should store the closure and drop it manually when appropriate.

Example: Handling an Input Field's Change Event

Suppose you want to respond to a user typing into an input field. First, the HTML:

```
<input id="name" type="text" />
```

Now in Rust:

```rust
use web_sys::{HtmlInputElement, Event};

#[wasm_bindgen(start)]
pub fn init_input_listener() -> Result<(), JsValue>
{
    let document =
web_sys::window().unwrap().document().unwrap();
    let input = document
        .get_element_by_id("name")
        .unwrap()
        .dyn_into::<HtmlInputElement>()
        .unwrap();

    let closure = Closure::wrap(Box::new(move
|event: Event| {
        let input = event
            .target()
            .unwrap()
            .dyn_into::<HtmlInputElement>()
            .unwrap();
        let value = input.value();
        web_sys::console::log_1(&format!("Typed:
{}", value).into());
    }) as Box<dyn FnMut(_)>);


input.set_oninput(Some(closure.as_ref().unchecked_r
ef()));
    closure.forget();
```

```
    Ok(())
}
```

In this case, the closure accepts an `Event` argument. We use `event.target()` to get the element that triggered the event, then convert it back into `HtmlInputElement` so we can read the value.

The closure is typed as `FnMut(_)` to allow for mutable captures or state updates. That's a key distinction in Rust—`Fn` is for closures that take no mutable references, `FnMut` allows mutation, and `FnOnce` consumes the environment.

Reusable Callback Utilities

In larger projects, repeating `Closure::wrap`, `unchecked_ref`, and `forget()` gets tedious. It's common to wrap these patterns into a utility function or a helper struct.

Here's an example utility function:

```
fn add_event_listener<E: wasm_bindgen::JsCast +
'static>(
    element: &E,
    event: &str,
    handler: impl FnMut(web_sys::Event) + 'static,
) {
    let closure = Closure::wrap(Box::new(handler)
as Box<dyn FnMut(_)>);
    let target = element
        .dyn_ref::<web_sys::EventTarget>()
        .expect("element should be an
EventTarget");

    target
        .add_event_listener_with_callback(event,
closure.as_ref().unchecked_ref())
        .unwrap();

    closure.forget(); // or store if you want to
remove later
}
```

You could now attach event handlers cleanly:

```
let input = document
    .get_element_by_id("name")
    .unwrap()
    .dyn_into::<HtmlInputElement>()
    .unwrap();

add_event_listener(&input, "input", move |event| {
    let input = event
        .target()
        .unwrap()
        .dyn_into::<HtmlInputElement>()
        .unwrap();
    console::log_1(&format!("Updated: {}",
input.value()).into());
});
```

This approach avoids repetitive boilerplate and lets you centralize memory management logic if you decide not to `.forget()` closures.

Removing Event Listeners

To remove an event listener, you must **retain a reference to the closure** you passed in. Without this, you can't call `remove_event_listener_with_callback`, because JavaScript compares references by identity.

Here's how to retain a closure:

```
let closure: Closure<dyn FnMut(_)> =
Closure::wrap(Box::new(move |e: Event| {
    // handle event
}));

element
    .add_event_listener_with_callback("click",
closure.as_ref().unchecked_ref())
    .unwrap();

// Later...
element
```

```
    .remove_event_listener_with_callback("click",
closure.as_ref().unchecked_ref())
    .unwrap();
```

You should **not** call `.forget()` in this case. Instead, store the `closure` in a `Rc<RefCell<Option<Closure<...>>>>` or similar container so you can drop it later.

Handling events and callbacks in Rust for WebAssembly involves a few important concepts:

- **Closures must be wrapped** with `Closure::wrap()` to be passed to JavaScript.
- **Memory must be managed explicitly**, either by calling `.forget()` to keep the closure alive or storing it for later use.
- **Event arguments must be cast** from generic `Event` types into specific DOM element types.
- **Ownership and lifetimes matter**, especially when dealing with dynamically triggered logic.

By mastering this workflow, you can build responsive, browser-integrated Rust applications that respond to user input and JavaScript events in a safe, performant way—without sacrificing the memory safety and control Rust is known for.

Passing Complex Data Structures Across the Boundary

When working with WebAssembly modules written in Rust and running inside a JavaScript host—typically a browser—you'll eventually need to exchange more than just strings, numbers, or booleans. Real applications involve **structured data**: objects, arrays, nested maps, and custom types. Bridging this data across the Rust–JavaScript boundary requires care, precision, and the right tooling.

Rust's type system is strict and static. JavaScript's is dynamic and flexible. To send complex data across the WebAssembly boundary, you must account for how memory is represented, how values are encoded, and how type conversions are handled.

The foundation for this exchange is `JsValue`, which represents any JavaScript value. But for structured data, we rely heavily on Serde—Rust's de facto serialization framework—and the `serde-wasm-bindgen` crate, which provides the glue for converting Rust types to and from `JsValue`.

Let's work through both directions: sending structured data from JavaScript into Rust, and returning structured Rust types back to JavaScript.

Receiving JavaScript Objects in Rust

Suppose you're working with a frontend where you gather form data in JavaScript and need to send it to a Rust function for validation or computation.

Here's the object you'll pass from JavaScript:

```
const user = {
   name: "Ada Lovelace",
   age: 36,
   email: "ada@example.com"
};
```

In Rust, define a matching structure with Serde's `Deserialize`:

```
use wasm_bindgen::prelude::*;
use serde::Deserialize;
use serde_wasm_bindgen;

#[derive(Deserialize)]
pub struct User {
    name: String,
    age: u32,
    email: String,
}

#[wasm_bindgen]
pub fn greet_user(js_val: JsValue) ->
Result<String, JsValue> {
    let user: User =
serde_wasm_bindgen::from_value(js_val)?;
    Ok(format!("Welcome, {}! You're {} years old.",
user.name, user.age))
}
```

This function:

- Accepts a `JsValue` from JavaScript.
- Uses `serde_wasm_bindgen::from_value` to convert it into a strongly typed Rust struct.
- Returns a formatted greeting string.

And here's how you'd use it from JavaScript:

```
const message = greet_user({
  name: "Ada Lovelace",
  age: 36,
  email: "ada@example.com"
});
console.log(message); // "Welcome, Ada Lovelace!
You're 36 years old."
```

This approach is safe and idiomatic. If the JavaScript object is missing a field or has a type mismatch, the deserialization fails, and a structured error is returned.

Sending Structured Rust Data Back to JavaScript

Now let's go the other direction. Suppose your Rust code computes something and returns a structured result—like a user profile or search result.

Define a Rust struct and derive `Serialize`:

```
use serde::Serialize;

#[derive(Serialize)]
pub struct Profile {
    username: String,
    score: u32,
    active: bool,
}

#[wasm_bindgen]
pub fn get_profile() -> JsValue {
    let profile = Profile {
        username: "rustacean".into(),
        score: 98,
```

```
        active: true,
    };
    serde_wasm_bindgen::to_value(&profile).unwrap()
}
```

JavaScript can now receive the result:

```
const profile = get_profile();
console.log(profile.username); // "rustacean"
console.log(profile.score);    // 98
console.log(profile.active);   // true
```

serde_wasm_bindgen::to_value() handles the conversion from the structured Rust type into a JsValue that behaves like a JavaScript object. The result supports property access, JSON serialization, and inspection like any other native object.

Working with Arrays of Structs

Suppose you're processing a list of structured records—perhaps user comments, search hits, or product data.

In Rust:

```
#[derive(Serialize)]
pub struct Comment {
    author: String,
    message: String,
}

#[wasm_bindgen]
pub fn get_comments() -> JsValue {
    let comments = vec![
        Comment {
            author: "Grace".to_string(),
            message: "This is
insightful!".to_string(),
        },
        Comment {
            author: "Linus".to_string(),
            message: "Thanks for the
explanation.".to_string(),
```

```
        },
    ];


serde_wasm_bindgen::to_value(&comments).unwrap()
}
```

In JavaScript:

```
const comments = get_comments();
comments.forEach(comment => {
   console.log(`[${comment.author}]
${comment.message}`);
});
```

Even though this is a `Vec<T>` in Rust, it becomes a native JavaScript array, with each item as a plain object. `serde-wasm-bindgen` takes care of all array boxing, memory layout, and ownership under the hood.

Nested Data Structures and Optional Fields

Rust's strong typing extends to deeply nested structures, enums, and optional values.

For example:

```
#[derive(Deserialize)]
pub struct Address {
    street: String,
    city: String,
}

#[derive(Deserialize)]
pub struct Person {
    name: String,
    age: u8,
    address: Option<Address>,
}
JavaScript:
const person = {
   name: "Dennis",
   age: 45,
```

```
  address: {
    street: "123 Kernel Rd",
    city: "Unixville"
  }
};

const result = process_person(person);
```

This pattern lets you safely represent both complete and partial data structures. If the address is missing, Option will automatically map it to None without causing a crash.

Error Handling for Deserialization

When using serde_wasm_bindgen::from_value(), any mismatch in types or structure results in an error. It's best to return Result<T, JsValue> and let the JavaScript caller handle it.

```
#[wasm_bindgen]
pub fn validate_user(input: JsValue) ->
Result<JsValue, JsValue> {
    let user: User =
serde_wasm_bindgen::from_value(input)?;

    if user.name.is_empty() {
        return Err(JsValue::from_str("Name cannot
be empty"));
    }

    Ok(JsValue::from_str("User is valid"))
}
```

From JavaScript:

```
try {
  validate_user({ name: "", age: 21 });
} catch (e) {
  console.error(e); // "Name cannot be empty"
}
```

This pattern ensures robustness in cases where the JavaScript caller passes incorrect or malformed data.

Passing complex data structures between Rust and JavaScript requires deliberate structure and clear type expectations. With `serde`, `serde_wasm_bindgen`, and `JsValue`, you can:

- Receive typed data from JavaScript into Rust safely.
- Return structured Rust objects as native JavaScript values.
- Work with lists, nested objects, enums, and optional fields easily.
- Handle errors cleanly without panics or unsafe behavior.

Once this interface is in place, Rust and JavaScript can collaborate cleanly—allowing you to build powerful, high-performance applications where business logic lives in Rust, and UI rendering and orchestration stay in JavaScript.

Chapter 5: Building Real Web Interfaces with Rust and Wasm

WebAssembly isn't just about performance or computational speed—it's also about **building usable interfaces**. In many cases, especially when working in the browser, your Rust code needs to not only run quickly but also respond to real users: update the UI, read form inputs, modify the DOM, and coordinate with frontend frameworks.

While JavaScript has native access to all browser APIs, Rust can reach these same capabilities through the `web-sys` crate, which exposes nearly the entire Web API surface in a type-safe, Rust-friendly manner. In this chapter, you'll learn how to directly manipulate the DOM with Rust, create basic interactive components, and even interoperate with popular JavaScript frontend frameworks like React or Vue when needed.

DOM Manipulation Using Rust

When writing frontend web applications, interacting with the DOM (Document Object Model) is a core activity. Whether it's updating text content, creating new elements, setting attributes, or responding to user actions, manipulating the DOM allows your application to reflect internal state and user interaction visually. Traditionally, this work is done in JavaScript. But with WebAssembly and Rust, you can take full control of DOM manipulation in a memory-safe, statically typed environment.

In Rust, you interact with the browser's DOM APIs using the `web-sys` crate, which exposes bindings to nearly the entire Web IDL surface. These bindings correspond directly to the methods and interfaces you'd use in JavaScript, but they're exposed in a way that integrates cleanly with Rust's type system and ownership model.

Accessing the Document and DOM Elements

To start, you'll typically obtain references to the browser's `window` and `document` objects using `web_sys::window()` and `document()`.

Here's the basic setup:

```
use web_sys::{window, Document, Element};

fn get_document() -> Document {
    window().expect("no global `window`
exists").document().expect("should have a
document")
}
```

Once you have the `Document`, you can access elements by ID, tag name, or selectors, similar to how you would in JavaScript.

Let's access an element by ID:

```
use wasm_bindgen::prelude::*;
use web_sys::HtmlElement;

#[wasm_bindgen]
pub fn update_title() -> Result<(), JsValue> {
    let document = get_document();
    let title = document
        .get_element_by_id("page-title")
        .expect("element not found")
        .dyn_into::<HtmlElement>()?;

    title.set_inner_text("Updated Title from
Rust");
    Ok(())
}
```

This function updates the text content of an element with the ID `page-title`. Note that `.dyn_into::<HtmlElement>()?` is used to downcast from the generic `Element` to a specific HTML element type.

Creating and Inserting Elements

You can create new DOM nodes in Rust and insert them into the document using methods like `create_element`, `append_child`, and `set_inner_html`.

Here's how to dynamically create and insert a paragraph into a `div` container:

```
use wasm_bindgen::prelude::*;
use web_sys::{Document, HtmlElement};
```

```
#[wasm_bindgen]
pub fn add_paragraph(text: &str) -> Result<(),
JsValue> {
    let document = get_document();
    let container = document
        .get_element_by_id("content")
        .expect("container not found");

    let paragraph = document.create_element("p")?;
    paragraph.set_text_content(Some(text));

    container.append_child(&paragraph)?;
    Ok(())
}
```

With this function, you can call `add_paragraph("This was added from Rust")` and a new paragraph will appear inside the container.

You can also assign CSS classes and set attributes:

```
paragraph.set_attribute("class", "highlight")?;
```

```
paragraph.set_attribute("data-id", "42")?;
```

Modifying Classes, Styles, and Attributes

Beyond setting inner text, you might want to add or remove classes, toggle visibility, or update inline styles. `web-sys` provides direct access to `class_list` and `style`.

```
use wasm_bindgen::JsCast;
use web_sys::HtmlElement;

#[wasm_bindgen]
pub fn toggle_visibility() -> Result<(), JsValue> {
    let document = get_document();
    let element = document
        .get_element_by_id("toggle-box")
        .unwrap()
        .dyn_into::<HtmlElement>()?;
```

```
    let current =
element.style().get_property_value("display")?;
    if current == "none" {
        element.style().set_property("display",
"block")?;
    } else {
        element.style().set_property("display",
"none")?;
    }

    Ok(())
}
```

This function toggles an element's visibility by changing its CSS `display` property.

To modify CSS classes:

```
let class_list = element.class_list();

class_list.add_1("visible")?;

class_list.remove_1("hidden")?;
```

This allows for dynamic styling purely from Rust.

Updating Input Fields and Reading Values

In interactive forms, you often need to both read user input and set field values programmatically.

To set the value of an `<input>` field:

```
use web_sys::HtmlInputElement;

#[wasm_bindgen]
pub fn set_input_value(new_value: &str) ->
Result<(), JsValue> {
    let document = get_document();
    let input = document
        .get_element_by_id("name-input")
        .unwrap()
```

```
        .dyn_into::<HtmlInputElement>()?;

    input.set_value(new_value);
    Ok(())
}
```

To read the value from the same input:

```
#[wasm_bindgen]
pub fn get_input_value() -> Result<JsValue,
JsValue> {
    let document = get_document();
    let input = document
        .get_element_by_id("name-input")
        .unwrap()
        .dyn_into::<HtmlInputElement>()?;

    Ok(JsValue::from_str(&input.value()))
}
```

This pattern is common in form processing, filtering, or creating live previews.

Practical Exercise: Dynamic Todo List

Here's a simple example that adds todo items to a list using Rust.

HTML:

```
<ul id="todo-list"></ul>
```

Rust:

```
#[wasm_bindgen]
pub fn add_todo(task: &str) -> Result<(), JsValue>
{
    let document = get_document();
    let list = document
        .get_element_by_id("todo-list")
        .unwrap();

    let item = document.create_element("li")?;
    item.set_inner_html(task);
```

```
    list.append_child(&item)?;
    Ok(())
}
```

Call this from JavaScript or from an event listener, and it will dynamically grow the list.

Rust, through WebAssembly and **web-sys**, offers full access to DOM manipulation capabilities traditionally reserved for JavaScript—without sacrificing performance or memory safety. You can:

- Access and modify DOM elements
- Create and inject new nodes
- Control classes, styles, and attributes
- Work with input and form elements
- Build dynamic, interactive UI behavior entirely from Rust

This isn't theoretical—these techniques scale to large, real applications. With a structured approach and careful use of web-sys, you can keep your application logic in Rust while still delivering responsive, browser-native experiences. In the next section, you'll see how to use these same tools to handle events and integrate with the broader browser environment.

Using web-sys to Access Browser APIs

When you compile Rust to WebAssembly for browser-based applications, your code runs in a secure sandbox that lacks access to the native operating system. But the browser itself provides a rich set of APIs—from basic DOM manipulation to canvas rendering, geolocation, local storage, and WebSockets. In JavaScript, these are available by default. In Rust, you gain access through the web-sys crate, which provides bindings to the Web APIs defined by the W3C's Web IDL.

web-sys is a comprehensive, auto-generated crate that allows Rust code to interact directly with the browser's JavaScript objects in a type-safe, low-overhead way. It is the foundation for browser-native Rust development.

Getting Access to window, document, and location

74

Many browser features start at the global `window` object. In Rust, use the `web_sys::window()` function, which returns an `Option<Window>`.

```
use web_sys::{window, Document, HtmlElement};

pub fn get_document() -> Document {
    window()
        .expect("should have a window")
        .document()
        .expect("window should have a document")
}
```

From this `Document`, you can query elements, create nodes, and control the entire structure of the page.

You can also access the current page's location:

```
use web_sys::Url;

pub fn get_current_path() -> String {
    let location = window().unwrap().location();
    location.pathname().unwrap_or_else(||
"/".to_string())
}
```

This works exactly like `window.location.pathname` in JavaScript.

Logging to the Console

The `console` API is one of the most basic debugging tools you'll need in any web application. `web-sys` provides bindings to all standard logging methods.

```
use web_sys::console;

pub fn log_message() {
    console::log_1(&"Logged from Rust!".into());
    console::warn_1(&"Warning from Rust!".into());
    console::error_1(&"Something went
wrong!".into());
}
```

These functions mirror the JavaScript console API (`console.log()`, `console.warn()`, etc.). You can pass in any `JsValue`, including strings, numbers, or objects.

Working with Canvas

To draw graphics in Rust using HTML5 canvas, use `web-sys` bindings for `CanvasRenderingContext2d`. Here's how to set up a basic drawing context.

HTML:

```
<canvas id="canvas" width="300"
height="150"></canvas>
```

Rust:

```rust
use wasm_bindgen::prelude::*;
use web_sys::{CanvasRenderingContext2d,
HtmlCanvasElement};

#[wasm_bindgen]
pub fn draw_circle() -> Result<(), JsValue> {
    let document = get_document();
    let canvas = document
        .get_element_by_id("canvas")
        .unwrap()
        .dyn_into::<HtmlCanvasElement>()?;

    let context = canvas
        .get_context("2d")?
        .unwrap()
        .dyn_into::<CanvasRenderingContext2d>()?;

    context.begin_path();
    context
        .arc(75.0, 75.0, 50.0, 0.0,
std::f64::consts::PI * 2.0)
        .unwrap();
    context.set_fill_style(&"blue".into());
    context.fill();

    Ok(())
```

```
}
```

This example draws a filled blue circle at the center of the canvas. All the method names, argument types, and return values match the JavaScript version, but with type checks enforced by Rust at compile time.

Using Local Storage and Session Storage

For persistent client-side storage, you can use the browser's `localStorage` or `sessionStorage`.

```
use web_sys::Storage;

pub fn save_to_storage(key: &str, value: &str) {
    let storage: Storage =
window().unwrap().local_storage().unwrap().unwrap()
;
    storage.set_item(key, value).unwrap();
}

pub fn load_from_storage(key: &str) ->
Option<String> {
    let storage: Storage =
window().unwrap().local_storage().unwrap().unwrap()
;
    storage.get_item(key).unwrap()
}
```

These bindings let you save strings that persist across page reloads. The storage API only works with strings, so if you're storing structured data, use `serde_json` to serialize it.

Using Timers: `setTimeout` and `setInterval`

The browser provides scheduling functions like `setTimeout` and `setInterval`. You can call them using closures in Rust.

```
use wasm_bindgen::closure::Closure;
use wasm_bindgen::JsCast;

pub fn schedule_log() {
    let callback = Closure::wrap(Box::new(move || {
```

```
        web_sys::console::log_1(&"Timer
triggered".into());
    }) as Box<dyn Fn()>);

    window()
        .unwrap()

.set_timeout_with_callback_and_timeout_and_argument
s_0(
            callback.as_ref().unchecked_ref(),
            2000,
        )
        .unwrap();

    callback.forget(); // Prevents Rust from
deallocating it
}
```

This will log a message after 2 seconds. The key point is using `.forget()` to keep the closure alive—otherwise, it would be dropped and deallocated, causing undefined behavior.

Using requestAnimationFrame

For smooth animation or frame-by-frame drawing, the browser's requestAnimationFrame is essential.

```
pub fn animate_once() {
    let callback = Closure::wrap(Box::new(move
|timestamp: f64| {
        web_sys::console::log_1(&format!("Animation
frame at {}", timestamp).into());
    }) as Box<dyn FnMut(f64)>);

    window()
        .unwrap()

.request_animation_frame(callback.as_ref().unchecke
d_ref())
        .unwrap();

    callback.forget();
```

```
}
```

This schedules a single animation frame callback. For continuous animations, you would need to call `requestAnimationFrame()` again inside the callback.

Working with Browser Events

Here's a quick example showing how to attach a click handler to a button:

HTML:

```
<button id="greet-btn">Greet</button>
```

Rust:

```rust
use web_sys::{HtmlElement, Event};

#[wasm_bindgen]
pub fn setup_button() -> Result<(), JsValue> {
    let document = get_document();
    let button = document
        .get_element_by_id("greet-btn")
        .unwrap()
        .dyn_into::<HtmlElement>()?;

    let closure = Closure::wrap(Box::new(move |_:
Event| {
        web_sys::console::log_1(&"Hello from
Rust!".into());
    }) as Box<dyn FnMut(_)>);


button.set_onclick(Some(closure.as_ref().unchecked_
ref()));
    closure.forget();

    Ok(())
}
```

This allows Rust to respond to browser events the same way JavaScript would.

`web-sys` unlocks full access to the browser from within your Rust WebAssembly modules. Whether you're working with:

- DOM manipulation
- Canvas drawing
- Browser storage
- Timing and animation
- Native events

—you can do it safely and efficiently with the same capabilities as JavaScript. The key differences are strong typing, memory safety, and explicit lifetime management, which give you more control and fewer bugs at runtime.

Using `web-sys`, you are not limited to computational logic. You can build entire interfaces, games, tools, or visualization layers directly in Rust, while still integrating seamlessly with the rest of the web platform.

Creating a Simple Interactive Frontend

Building interactive user interfaces with Rust and WebAssembly is not just possible—it's practical. While Rust doesn't have built-in support for reactive rendering or declarative UI like React or Vue, it gives you the tools to create highly interactive browser-based applications by manipulating the DOM directly and responding to user input in real time.

In this section, you'll build a small yet complete frontend entirely in Rust, compiled to WebAssembly. This frontend will handle state, user interaction, and UI updates—all with the safety and clarity of Rust's type system.

Goal: A Clickable Counter Interface

The application you'll build is a simple counter. It will:

- Display a number in the browser
- Include two buttons: one to increment the count, another to reset it
- Update the DOM dynamically based on user input

This will demonstrate essential skills: accessing elements, managing state, responding to events, and updating content—all from Rust.

Step 1: HTML Setup

The HTML defines the structure of the page. It will be static; Rust will handle the logic and behavior.

```html
<!DOCTYPE html>
<html lang="en">
<head>
  <meta charset="UTF-8">
  <title>Rust Wasm Counter</title>
</head>
<body>
  <h1>Counter</h1>
  <p id="counter">0</p>
  <button id="inc">+1</button>
  <button id="reset">Reset</button>

  <script type="module">
    import init from
'./pkg/interactive_frontend.js';
    init(); // Initialize the Wasm module
  </script>
</body>
</html>
```

This HTML page has an element to display the counter (`<p id="counter">`) and two buttons to interact with the application.

Step 2: Rust Code

Create a new Rust project with `wasm-pack`:

```
wasm-pack new interactive_frontend

cd interactive_frontend
```

Edit `src/lib.rs`:

```rust
use wasm_bindgen::prelude::*;
use wasm_bindgen::JsCast;
use web_sys::{window, Document, HtmlElement};
use std::cell::RefCell;
use std::rc::Rc;
```

```rust
#[wasm_bindgen(start)]
pub fn run() -> Result<(), JsValue> {
    let document: Document =
window().unwrap().document().unwrap();

    let counter_display = document
        .get_element_by_id("counter")
        .unwrap()
        .dyn_into::<HtmlElement>()?;

    let count = Rc::new(RefCell::new(0));

    {
        let count = count.clone();
        let counter_display =
counter_display.clone();

        let inc_button =
document.get_element_by_id("inc").unwrap();
        let closure = Closure::wrap(Box::new(move
|| {
            *count.borrow_mut() += 1;

counter_display.set_inner_text(&count.borrow().to_s
tring());
        }) as Box<dyn Fn()>);

        inc_button
            .dyn_into::<HtmlElement>()?

.set_onclick(Some(closure.as_ref().unchecked_ref())
);
        closure.forget();
    }

    {
        let count = count.clone();
        let counter_display =
counter_display.clone();

        let reset_button =
document.get_element_by_id("reset").unwrap();
```

```
        let closure = Closure::wrap(Box::new(move
|| {

            *count.borrow_mut() = 0;
            counter_display.set_inner_text("0");
        }) as Box<dyn Fn()>);

        reset_button
            .dyn_into::<HtmlElement>()?

.set_onclick(Some(closure.as_ref().unchecked_ref())
);
        closure.forget();
    }

    Ok(())
}
```

Here's what this does, step-by-step:

1. **Access the DOM** using `window()` and `document()` to find the counter display and buttons by ID.
2. **Manage state** using `Rc<RefCell<i32>>` to allow shared, mutable access between closures.
3. **Create closures** for the +1 and `Reset` buttons, updating the shared count and updating the DOM accordingly.
4. **Attach event handlers** using `set_onclick`, passing the closures after converting them to JavaScript-compatible references.
5. **Prevent deallocation** using `.forget()` so the closures persist after the Rust function returns.

This program is self-contained. Once compiled with `wasm-pack`, it produces a WebAssembly module with JavaScript bindings that can be imported into your HTML page.

Step 3: Build with wasm-pack

Compile the project:

```
wasm-pack build --target web
```

This creates a `pkg/` folder containing a `.wasm` binary and the JavaScript glue code needed to call your Rust functions from a browser.

Copy the contents of your `pkg/` folder into a directory served by a static web server, alongside your HTML file.

You can test the result with any static server, such as `serve`:

```
npm install -g serve

serve .
```

Then open `http://localhost:3000` and interact with your counter.

What This Demonstrates

- **DOM interaction** in Rust using `web-sys`
- **State management** in Rust without any JavaScript frameworks
- **Memory safety** even in the face of closures and shared state
- **Cross-boundary event handling**, calling Rust closures from native browser events

Practical Tips

1. **Use `Rc<RefCell<T>>`** for any shared state that needs to be updated across closures.
2. **Avoid forgetting closures unless necessary.** If you need to remove event listeners, you'll want to retain references and avoid `.forget()`.
3. **Leverage `wasm_bindgen(start)`** to automatically initialize your module on page load.
4. **Use `.dyn_into::<...>()` safely.** Always check or expect that you're downcasting the right type.
5. **Wrap complex logic** into reusable functions as your UI grows.

This simple counter illustrates the fundamentals of creating interactive frontends in Rust using WebAssembly. You directly control DOM elements, respond to user actions with closures, and manage state using standard Rust patterns—all without relying on JavaScript frameworks or toolchains.

From this foundation, you can grow your UI to handle forms, dynamic lists, or even integrate into a larger JavaScript-based application. The key takeaway is that **Rust is not just a backend tool**—with WebAssembly and the right browser bindings, it's a viable and powerful frontend option.

Integrating with JavaScript Frameworks

WebAssembly and Rust are not designed to replace JavaScript in frontend development. Instead, they are ideal for **augmenting** existing JavaScript-based applications—especially when performance, safety, or low-level control is needed. In practice, this means embedding Rust-generated WebAssembly modules into modern frameworks like React, Vue, Svelte, Angular, or even plain JavaScript projects. The integration is direct and efficient because Rust compiles to .wasm, and wasm-bindgen and wasm-pack generate idiomatic JavaScript bindings.

Preparing a Rust Library for Integration

Start with a Rust crate built for WebAssembly. Here's a basic example of a Rust function you want to use in your frontend:

```
// src/lib.rs

use wasm_bindgen::prelude::*;

#[wasm_bindgen]
pub fn double(x: i32) -> i32 {
    x * 2
}
```

This function is marked with #[wasm_bindgen] so that it can be exposed to JavaScript.

Build it using:

```
wasm-pack build --target bundler
```

This produces a pkg/ folder with a .wasm file and JavaScript bindings you can import into any JS/TS project using modern bundlers like Vite, Webpack, or Rollup.

Example: Using Rust in a React Component

Here's how to integrate this into a React component.

Install the Rust package locally or copy the `pkg/` folder into your React project.

File structure:

```
my-react-app/
├── src/
│    ├── App.jsx
│    └── ...
├── pkg/
│    ├── my_wasm_module_bg.wasm
│    └── my_wasm_module.js
└── index.html
```

App.jsx:

```jsx
import React, { useEffect, useState } from "react";
import init, { double } from
"../pkg/my_wasm_module";

function App() {
  const [value, setValue] = useState(2);
  const [result, setResult] = useState(null);

  useEffect(() => {
    init(); // Load the WASM module once on
component mount
  }, []);

  const handleClick = () => {
    setResult(double(value));
  };

  return (
    <div>
      <input
        type="number"
        value={value}
        onChange={e =>
setValue(parseInt(e.target.value, 10))}
      />
      <button onClick={handleClick}>Double</button>
```

```
      {result !== null && <p>Result from Rust:
{result}</p>}
    </div>
  );
}

export default App;
```

This React component uses `useState` to hold a number, calls a Rust function when the button is clicked, and displays the result. The `init()` function is generated by `wasm-bindgen` and is required to instantiate the `.wasm` binary before any Rust functions are called.

Example: Using Rust with Vue 3

To integrate Rust with Vue, follow the same approach—compile your `.wasm` module with `wasm-pack`, and import it in a Vue component.

Vue Single File Component:

```
<template>
  <div>
    <input v-model.number="num" type="number" />
    <button @click="run">Double</button>
    <p v-if="result !== null">Result from Rust: {{
result }}</p>
  </div>
</template>

<script setup>
import { ref, onMounted } from 'vue'
import init, { double } from
'../pkg/my_wasm_module'

const num = ref(5)
const result = ref(null)

onMounted(async () => {
  await init()
})

function run() {
```

```
    result.value = double(num.value)
}
</script>
```

This Vue component uses Composition API (`ref`, `onMounted`) and binds the input to a number. On button click, it calls the Rust function and updates the DOM with the result.

Exposing Complex Rust Functions to Frameworks

You're not limited to simple math. You can also return strings, JSON-like structures, or even use `serde` to decode/encode objects.

Rust:

```rust
use wasm_bindgen::prelude::*;
use serde::{Deserialize, Serialize};

#[derive(Serialize, Deserialize)]
pub struct User {
    name: String,
    age: u8,
}

#[wasm_bindgen]
pub fn greet_user(user: JsValue) -> Result<JsValue,
JsValue> {
    let user: User = user.into_serde().map_err(|e|
e.to_string())?;
    let msg = format!("Hello, {}, age {}",
user.name, user.age);
    Ok(JsValue::from_str(&msg))
}
```

React Example:

```javascript
const user = { name: "Grace", age: 30 };

const message = greet_user(user);

console.log(message); // "Hello, Grace, age 30"
```

You can now pass JavaScript objects to Rust, have Rust validate or transform the data, and return structured results.

Using TypeScript with Rust-Wasm

`wasm-pack` can generate TypeScript definitions when using:

```
wasm-pack build --target bundler --typescript
```

This gives you `*.d.ts` files in your `pkg/` folder, enabling full IntelliSense in IDEs and better safety when working in TypeScript-heavy frameworks.

In TypeScript (e.g. in SvelteKit or Angular):

```
import init, { greet_user } from
"../pkg/my_wasm_module"

await init()
const msg = greet_user({ name: "Ada", age: 28 }) as
string
```

TypeScript will now treat `greet_user` as a typed function, improving dev experience.

Deployment Considerations

When integrating Rust with JavaScript frameworks:

- **Preload the .wasm file** during app initialization (via `init()`).
- **Use code splitting** to lazy-load modules if needed.
- **Minify with production flags** using `wasm-pack build --release`.
- **Handle errors gracefully**, especially if deserialization or bindings fail.

Real-World Applications

Rust-Wasm modules are particularly useful in frontend apps when:

- You need to run cryptographic functions (e.g. hashing, signature verification)

- You need to parse and validate complex structured data (e.g. schemas, formats)
- You want to isolate sensitive logic from JavaScript (e.g. license verification)
- You're building a plugin for a larger web-based platform

The key is modularity: you can write and test the logic in Rust, compile to Wasm, and drop it into your frontend codebase like any other module.

Rust and JavaScript frameworks **can coexist cleanly**. By compiling Rust functions into Wasm and using `wasm-bindgen` to expose them, you can call those functions directly from modern frontend libraries like React, Vue, and Svelte. This enables performance-critical logic to be written in Rust while allowing the rest of your app to use the reactive UI and ecosystem tooling you're already familiar with.

This hybrid model is highly maintainable, portable, and efficient—letting you push the limits of browser performance without abandoning modern frontend development workflows.

Chapter 6: Performance Optimization in Rust-Wasm Apps

Building Rust applications that run in the browser using WebAssembly unlocks an incredible level of performance, safety, and cross-platform flexibility. But to fully benefit from these strengths, you need to **optimize your Wasm binaries and code execution paths**. Without attention to detail, it's easy to introduce unnecessary overhead—from bloated output files to redundant bindings—that can slow down load times and undermine the performance gains Rust is meant to deliver.

Memory Layout and Allocation Strategies

When writing WebAssembly applications in Rust, performance depends heavily on how you manage memory. Unlike JavaScript, which relies on a garbage-collected heap with hidden costs, Rust uses **explicit, deterministic memory allocation**. And when you compile to Wasm, your application operates inside a **linear memory buffer**, which behaves like a contiguous array of bytes. Understanding how memory is laid out and allocated in this model is essential if you want to avoid unnecessary overhead, control memory usage, and keep performance tight.

WebAssembly provides a flat, contiguous memory buffer. This memory is defined in **pages**, where each page is 64KiB in size. Memory is accessed by byte offsets. From Rust's perspective, this memory is abstracted and managed using pointers, slices, and heap-allocated structures like `Vec`, `Box`, and `String`.

When you compile Rust code to WebAssembly, memory is managed using a standard allocator (usually `dlmalloc`) unless you specify otherwise. All dynamic memory usage—heap allocation—happens inside the linear memory buffer. The more you allocate and retain, the larger this memory becomes.

To view and inspect this memory, modern browsers (like Chrome) let you open a live memory viewer under DevTools → Sources → WebAssembly → Memory. You'll see a raw byte buffer, and it grows in 64KiB pages as your app requests more heap space.

Choosing the Right Allocator for Wasm

Rust allows you to define a global allocator. The default `dlmalloc` allocator is general-purpose and efficient but includes a lot of logic you don't need when targeting the Web. For Wasm builds, you typically want something smaller—especially if you're optimizing for binary size.

The most popular lightweight allocator for Wasm is `wee_alloc`. It's a minimal global allocator designed specifically to reduce Wasm size.

Add it to `Cargo.toml`:

```
[dependencies]

wee_alloc = "0.4"
```

Enable it in your crate:

```
use wee_alloc::WeeAlloc;

#[global_allocator]
static ALLOC: WeeAlloc = WeeAlloc::INIT;
```

This swaps the default allocator with a version that has almost no internal fragmentation logic, minimal metadata, and a smaller code footprint—ideal for small-to-medium Wasm applications.

Understanding Stack and Heap Allocation in Wasm

Just like in native Rust, Wasm distinguishes between **stack** and **heap** memory:

- **Stack allocations** are fast and cheap. Local variables (e.g., arrays of known size, integers, fixed structs) live on the stack.
- **Heap allocations** occur when you create dynamic data (e.g., `String`, `Vec`, `Box`, `Rc`). These are slower, require bookkeeping, and live in the linear memory's heap segment.

Use the stack when possible for small, short-lived data. For example:

```
#[wasm_bindgen]
pub fn compute_sum() -> i32 {
    let data = [1, 2, 3, 4, 5]; // allocated on the stack
    data.iter().sum()
```

```
}
```

But if you do something like:

```rust
#[wasm_bindgen]
pub fn allocate_data() -> Vec<i32> {
    vec![1, 2, 3, 4, 5] // allocated on the heap
}
```

Then you are invoking the allocator, which increases your Wasm module's memory usage and startup time.

Pre-allocating and Reusing Buffers

To avoid repeated allocations—especially in high-frequency or performance-sensitive code—you should **preallocate memory and reuse it**.

Suppose you're writing a function that processes a large array of numbers every frame:

```rust
#[wasm_bindgen]
pub struct Processor {
    buffer: Vec<f32>,
}

#[wasm_bindgen]
impl Processor {
    #[wasm_bindgen(constructor)]
    pub fn new(size: usize) -> Processor {
        Processor {
            buffer: vec![0.0; size],
        }
    }

    pub fn update(&mut self, data: &[f32]) {
        for (i, &value) in data.iter().enumerate()
{
            self.buffer[i] = value * 2.0;
        }
    }

    pub fn get(&self) -> *const f32 {
```

```
        self.buffer.as_ptr()
    }

    pub fn len(&self) -> usize {
        self.buffer.len()
    }
}
```

Here, the buffer is allocated once during construction and reused in every `update` call. This avoids expensive heap growth and unnecessary zeroing of memory on every frame.

You can access the data in JavaScript using `wasm_memory.buffer`, slicing the data using the pointer and length.

Avoiding Fragmentation with Predictable Patterns

Heap fragmentation can occur when you create and drop many small objects over time. Although `wee_alloc` is very basic, this can still lead to slow memory growth in long-running apps.

To prevent this:

- Reuse `Vec<T>` by clearing instead of recreating:
- `self.buffer.clear(); // keeps capacity`
- Avoid repeated `String::from()` or `format!()` calls in hot paths.
- Don't hold short-lived `Box<T>` unless you need dynamic dispatch.

If you're allocating short-lived structures frequently, use **stack-based iterators**, fixed-size arrays, or even a static pool for reuse.

Observing Memory Growth in the Browser

You can inspect memory growth live in Chrome DevTools:

1. Open the "Memory" tab.
2. Trigger GC manually to remove JS memory from the chart.
3. Watch for Wasm memory usage.
4. Set breakpoints inside exported Rust functions.
5. Use `console.log(memory.buffer.byteLength)` in JS.

Also, consider exposing a function from Rust to log current page count:

```
#[wasm_bindgen]
pub fn memory_pages() -> u32 {

wasm_bindgen::memory().dyn_into::<web_sys::WebAssem
blyMemory>().unwrap().buffer().byte_length() as u32
/ 65536
}
```

This helps debug unexpected memory usage over time.

Best Practices Summary

- Use `wee_alloc` to reduce code size and overhead.
- Keep frequently reused buffers alive—allocate once, reuse many times.
- Minimize string creation, formatting, and cloning inside loops.
- Benchmark allocation cost using browser tools (performance tab + timeline).
- Prefer `clear()` over reallocating `Vec`s where feasible.
- Limit the use of `#[wasm_bindgen]` exports for private helper functions to reduce glue code and surface area.

Your Rust code compiled to Wasm shares one memory space: a flat, mutable, and expandable linear buffer. Every heap allocation touches this buffer. How you structure your data, choose your allocator, and manage reuse directly impacts binary size, execution speed, and browser performance.

By applying thoughtful memory layout and allocation strategies—using the right allocator, avoiding unnecessary heap growth, reusing memory buffers—you can ensure that your Rust-Wasm applications are as fast and efficient in the browser as they are in native environments.

Optimizing Binary Size with `wasm-opt`

When you compile Rust code to WebAssembly, the resulting `.wasm` binary includes not only your application logic but also allocator metadata, panic handlers, unused type information, and glue code generated by `wasm-bindgen`. Without post-processing, these binaries are significantly larger than necessary for production. Large WebAssembly binaries result in longer download times, slower startup, and higher memory usage in the browser.

To reduce binary size efficiently, you need to apply a tool specifically designed for WebAssembly optimization: `wasm-opt`. This tool analyzes the binary, removes redundancies, merges instructions, strips metadata, and applies deep compression strategies that go far beyond what `rustc` or `wasm-pack` can achieve alone.

Installing `wasm-opt`

`wasm-opt` is part of the Binaryen toolkit. It's cross-platform and can be installed easily:

On macOS (using Homebrew):

```
brew install binaryen
```

On Ubuntu/Debian:

```
sudo apt install binaryen
```

Via prebuilt binaries:

Download from the GitHub releases page, extract, and add to your system's path.

Once installed, verify it with:

```
wasm-opt --version
```

Using `wasm-opt` to Reduce Binary Size

After building your `.wasm` binary with `wasm-pack` in release mode, you'll get a file such as `pkg/my_project_bg.wasm`.

To optimize it, run:

```
wasm-opt -Oz -o pkg/my_project_bg.wasm
pkg/my_project_bg.wasm
```

This overwrites the original Wasm file with an optimized version.

Explanation of flags:

- `-Oz`: Optimize for size aggressively.
- `-O3`: Optimize for speed. Use this only if performance is more critical than file size.
- `--strip-debug`: Remove debug symbols.
- `--strip-producers`: Remove producer metadata (e.g., toolchain/version info).

Example full command:

```
wasm-opt -Oz --strip-debug --strip-producers -o
pkg/my_project_bg.wasm pkg/my_project_bg.wasm
```

This is safe to use on all production builds and can shrink binaries by **30–70%**, especially when combined with `wee_alloc` and release mode.

Example: Before vs After

Let's say you built your project with:

```
wasm-pack build --release
```

Initial binary size:

```
ls -lh pkg/my_project_bg.wasm
# 170 KB
```

Then optimize:

```
wasm-opt -Oz --strip-debug --strip-producers -o
pkg/my_project_bg.wasm pkg/my_project_bg.wasm
```

After optimization:

```
ls -lh pkg/my_project_bg.wasm
# 57 KB
```

That's a **66% reduction** in size, with no change in functionality.

Integrating into Build Workflows

You should always run `wasm-opt` as part of your production build process. You can do this manually or automate it.

Option 1: Bash Script

Create a `build.sh` file:

```bash
#!/bin/bash
set -e

wasm-pack build --release
wasm-opt -Oz --strip-debug --strip-producers -o
pkg/my_project_bg.wasm pkg/my_project_bg.wasm
```

Option 2: npm script (if using JS bundlers)

Update your `package.json`:

```json
"scripts": {
  "build": "wasm-pack build --release && wasm-opt -
Oz --strip-debug -o pkg/my_project_bg.wasm
pkg/my_project_bg.wasm"
}
```

Now run `npm run build` to compile and optimize in one step.

Enabling Link-Time Optimizations in Rust

For `wasm-opt` to be most effective, your binary needs to be slim to begin with. Set this in `Cargo.toml`:

```toml
[profile.release]
opt-level = "z"          # Optimize for size
lto = true               # Link-time optimization
codegen-units = 1      # Fewer units = better size reduction
```

This ensures the smallest possible `.wasm` is produced before post-processing.

Additional Tips

- Use **wee_alloc** to shrink allocator overhead.
- **Avoid std::fmt and format!** in hot paths—they pull in large format machinery.
- **Minimize #[wasm_bindgen] exports**—only expose what JavaScript needs.
- **Use --target bundler** if your frontend is using Webpack, Vite, or Rollup.
- **Bundle wasm-opt in CI** to enforce consistent optimization during deployment.

Troubleshooting

If `wasm-opt` fails or produces unexpected behavior:

1. Make sure your `.wasm` is a valid build artifact (run `wasm-validate` if needed).
2. Check for panics in Rust code—unhandled panics can embed large symbol tables.
3. Verify that no JS loader is caching the old `.wasm` file (try a hard refresh).
4. Avoid double-running `wasm-opt`—only process a binary once per build.

Optimizing your Wasm binary with `wasm-opt` is not optional—it's essential. A large `.wasm` file increases load time, drains bandwidth, and delays execution. `wasm-opt` provides a fast, reliable way to compress and polish your Rust-Wasm builds, with full control over size vs performance trade-offs.

By integrating `wasm-opt` into your build system, choosing the right flags, and combining it with size-conscious Rust patterns, you ensure your applications are fast not just at runtime—but also from the moment they're downloaded. In modern frontend performance, that's often the difference between success and abandonment.

Avoiding Unnecessary Bindings

One of the most overlooked causes of bloated WebAssembly binaries in Rust is exporting too much to JavaScript. Every time you mark a Rust function, struct, enum, or constant with #[wasm_bindgen], it generates extra glue code in both the `.wasm` binary and the associated JavaScript file. This glue includes metadata, type conversion logic, and allocation management. If you're not careful, your application may ship a large interface full of unused exports, increasing load time and memory use without adding value.

When you annotate a function with `#[wasm_bindgen]`, you're telling Rust to expose that function to the JavaScript side. This doesn't just export a raw pointer—it sets up:

- JavaScript wrapper functions
- Type conversion logic (e.g., strings ↔ `JsValue`)
- Memory handling across the boundary
- Metadata to describe the export in the `.wasm` binary

Here's a basic example:

```rust
#[wasm_bindgen]
pub fn add(a: i32, b: i32) -> i32 {
    a + b
}
```

This function is simple, but `wasm-bindgen` still has to wrap it in JavaScript glue code, ensure type compatibility, and expose it to JS as a callable function. The more functions you export, the more glue code is generated.

Rule 1: Export Only What JavaScript Needs

Your Rust crate may have dozens of helper functions, data processing routines, and utility methods. But unless they are directly called from JavaScript, they should **not be marked with** `#[wasm_bindgen]`.

Let's say you have this setup:

```rust
#[wasm_bindgen]
pub fn compute_something(data: Vec<f64>) -> f64 {
    let squared = square_all(&data);
    mean(&squared)
}

#[wasm_bindgen]
pub fn square_all(data: &Vec<f64>) -> Vec<f64> {
    data.iter().map(|x| x * x).collect()
}
```

```rust
#[wasm_bindgen]
pub fn mean(data: &Vec<f64>) -> f64 {
    let sum: f64 = data.iter().sum();
    sum / data.len() as f64
}
```

All three functions are exported to JavaScript, but only `compute_something` is called externally. The rest are internal helpers. Exporting them adds unnecessary bindings.

You should refactor it like this:

```rust
#[wasm_bindgen]
pub fn compute_something(data: Vec<f64>) -> f64 {
    let squared = square_all(&data);
    mean(&squared)
}

fn square_all(data: &Vec<f64>) -> Vec<f64> {
    data.iter().map(|x| x * x).collect()
}

fn mean(data: &Vec<f64>) -> f64 {
    let sum: f64 = data.iter().sum();
    sum / data.len() as f64
}
```

Now only one function is exported, and the others remain private to Rust, keeping the interface clean and the glue code minimal.

Rule 2: Avoid Exporting Structs Unless Necessary

When you mark a Rust `struct` with `#[wasm_bindgen]`, it creates a corresponding JavaScript class wrapper with constructor logic, methods, and allocation behavior. This is useful when your app's JavaScript side needs to instantiate Rust types and retain references—but in many cases, you can **hide complex types behind simple function-based interfaces**.

Example of unnecessary binding:

```rust
#[wasm_bindgen]
```

```rust
pub struct Rectangle {
    width: f64,
    height: f64,
}

#[wasm_bindgen]
impl Rectangle {
    pub fn area(&self) -> f64 {
        self.width * self.height
    }
}
```

If you're only using `Rectangle` within a single function, there's no need to expose it at all. Instead:

```rust
struct Rectangle {
    width: f64,
    height: f64,
}

impl Rectangle {
    fn area(&self) -> f64 {
        self.width * self.height
    }
}

#[wasm_bindgen]
pub fn compute_area(w: f64, h: f64) -> f64 {
    let rect = Rectangle { width: w, height: h };
    rect.area()
}
```

This avoids exporting the struct and reduces your `.wasm` file size while maintaining the same functionality.

Rule 3: Use `JsValue` Carefully

While `JsValue` is flexible and often necessary, it introduces generic conversion code that must be shipped with your binary. If you can stick to primitive types—`i32`, `f64`, `bool`, `String`, and `&[u8]`—you avoid expensive conversions.

Instead of:

```
#[wasm_bindgen]
pub fn greet(user: JsValue) -> JsValue {
    let name: String = js_sys::Reflect::get(&user,
&JsValue::from_str("name"))
        .unwrap()
        .as_string()
        .unwrap();

    JsValue::from_str(&format!("Hello, {}", name))
}
```

Prefer:

```
#[wasm_bindgen]
pub fn greet(name: &str) -> String {
    format!("Hello, {}", name)
}
```

This reduces glue complexity and memory allocation overhead.

If you need to pass structured data, use `serde` with `serde-wasm-bindgen` for serialization/deserialization, and avoid writing raw `JsValue` manipulation by hand.

Rule 4: Bundle Internal Logic into Higher-Level Exports

Instead of exporting many small pieces, group logic into fewer, higher-level entry points.

Bad:

```
#[wasm_bindgen] pub fn init() {}

#[wasm_bindgen] pub fn set_input(input: &str) {}

#[wasm_bindgen] pub fn process() -> String {}

#[wasm_bindgen] pub fn get_status() -> String {}
```

Better:

```
#[wasm_bindgen]
pub fn run_pipeline(input: &str) -> String {
    // internally call: init, set_input, process,
get_status
    process_input(input)
}
```

Fewer exports mean less glue code, simpler APIs, and better encapsulation. This approach also helps reduce the number of heap allocations shared between Rust and JS.

Verifying Exported Bindings

After building with `wasm-pack build`, inspect what's actually exported:

```
wasm-objdump -x pkg/your_project_bg.wasm | grep
export
```

Or use `wasm-tools`:

```
wasm-tools inspect pkg/your_project_bg.wasm
```

This helps you audit and ensure you aren't shipping extra functions unintentionally.

Real-World Example

Let's say you're building a Rust-based markdown renderer. Your naïve interface might expose functions like:

```
#[wasm_bindgen]
pub fn parse(input: &str) -> Vec<Token> {}
#[wasm_bindgen]
pub fn render(tokens: Vec<Token>) -> String {}
```

But unless JavaScript explicitly works with `Token`, you're better off hiding that:

```
fn parse(input: &str) -> Vec<Token> {
    // parsing logic...
}
```

```
fn render(tokens: Vec<Token>) -> String {
    // rendering logic...
}

#[wasm_bindgen]
pub fn render_markdown(input: &str) -> String {
    let tokens = parse(input);
    render(tokens)
}
```

The result is fewer bindings, smaller binaries, and no wasted metadata for the `Token` type in JS.

Avoiding unnecessary bindings in Rust-Wasm projects leads to **smaller binaries, faster load times**, and **simpler JavaScript integration**. To do this effectively:

- Export only the functions needed by JavaScript.
- Keep helpers, internal logic, and types private to Rust.
- Group functionality into fewer high-level entry points.
- Use primitive types when possible to reduce conversion overhead.
- Audit your exports regularly to keep the surface area lean.

The less you expose, the more optimized and maintainable your application becomes—both at the binary level and in the architecture of your interface between Rust and JavaScript.

Benchmarking Rust and JavaScript

When using Rust and WebAssembly in frontend development, one of the most important—and often misunderstood—questions is: *Is it faster than JavaScript?* The answer depends entirely on **how** you're using Rust, **what** you're benchmarking, and **where** the performance bottlenecks are. WebAssembly does offer significant performance advantages, but not universally. For tasks with tight computation loops, numerical processing, or predictable memory access patterns, Rust can dramatically outperform JavaScript. For tasks involving a lot of DOM manipulation, dynamic dispatch, or boundary crossings, JavaScript might be faster or at least more ergonomic.

Benchmarking is not about confirming assumptions—it's about measuring what actually happens in the browser under realistic conditions. This section guides you through designing meaningful benchmarks, running them in the browser, interpreting the results, and deciding where Rust gives you measurable gains.

Designing Meaningful Benchmarks

Before writing any code, define what you're comparing:

- **Is the logic CPU-bound or I/O-bound?**
- **How much time is spent inside Rust vs crossing the JS ↔ Wasm boundary?**
- **Is the data layout friendly to Wasm (typed, numeric, contiguous)?**
- **How does performance scale with input size?**

To benchmark properly, avoid synthetic "micro-benchmarks" unless your use case is micro-scale. Instead, choose **representative workloads** based on your actual application requirements.

Examples of suitable benchmarks include:

- Parsing large JSON data
- Computing FFT or matrix multiplications
- Hashing or encryption operations
- Running simulations or physics steps
- Complex string or number crunching

Setting Up the Benchmarking Environment

Let's create a simple benchmark that compares Rust and JavaScript functions side-by-side in the browser.

Rust (`src/lib.rs`):

```
use wasm_bindgen::prelude::*;

#[wasm_bindgen]
pub fn rust_sum(n: u32) -> u64 {
    (0..n).map(|x| x as u64).sum()
}
```

This function sums integers from 0 to n - 1. It's purely CPU-bound and uses a predictable, fast loop.

Build with:

```
wasm-pack build --release --target bundler
```

This produces the .wasm file and JS wrapper.

JavaScript Baseline Implementation

In your frontend JS or React/Vue/Svelte app:

```
function jsSum(n) {
   let total = 0;
   for (let i = 0; i < n; i++) {
     total += i;
   }
   return total;
}
```

This is semantically equivalent to the Rust function. Now let's benchmark both.

Running the Benchmark

Use the built-in console.time() and console.timeEnd() for a quick and practical benchmark in the browser.

HTML/JS:

```
<script type="module">
   import init, { rust_sum } from
"./pkg/your_module_name.js";

   async function runBenchmarks() {
     await init(); // load wasm

     const N = 100_000_000;

     console.time("JavaScript Sum");
     const jsResult = jsSum(N);
```

```
    console.timeEnd("JavaScript Sum");

    console.time("Rust/Wasm Sum");
    const rustResult = rust_sum(N);
    console.timeEnd("Rust/Wasm Sum");

    console.log({ jsResult, rustResult });
  }

  function jsSum(n) {
    let total = 0;
    for (let i = 0; i < n; i++) {
      total += i;
    }
    return total;
  }

  runBenchmarks();
</script>
```

Open DevTools (F12), go to the Console, and observe the timing output.

Real-World Example: Text Hashing

Let's test SHA-256 hash performance using both JavaScript (via Web Crypto) and Rust (via sha2 crate).

Rust (lib.rs):

```
use wasm_bindgen::prelude::*;
use sha2::{Sha256, Digest};

#[wasm_bindgen]
pub fn hash_data(data: &str) -> String {
    let mut hasher = Sha256::new();
    hasher.update(data.as_bytes());
    let result = hasher.finalize();
    hex::encode(result)
}
```

JavaScript:

```
async function jsHash(data) {

  const encoder = new TextEncoder();

  const hashBuffer = await
crypto.subtle.digest("SHA-256",
encoder.encode(data));

  return [...new Uint8Array(hashBuffer)].map(x =>
x.toString(16).padStart(2, "0")).join("");
}
```

Benchmark:

```
const input = "a".repeat(10_000_000);


console.time("JavaScript Hash");

await jsHash(input);

console.timeEnd("JavaScript Hash");


console.time("Rust Hash");

hash_data(input); // assumes init() is done

console.timeEnd("Rust Hash");
```

Results may show Rust is consistently faster—especially as input size increases. That's because Rust avoids JS-to-native string encoding and doesn't rely on the browser's internal async Crypto implementation.

Interpreting Results Correctly

- **Short operations** may perform worse in Rust due to boundary cost (JS ↔ Wasm).
- **Large workloads** benefit from Rust's compiled performance and zero-cost abstraction.

- **Heap allocation and string handling** add overhead to Wasm, especially if JS strings are passed repeatedly.
- **Crossing the boundary often** is expensive. Prefer batching and processing large inputs at once.

Use these insights to decide *when* it's worth moving logic from JavaScript to Rust:

Profiling With DevTools

Beyond `console.time()`, use **Chrome DevTools > Performance** tab:

1. Click "Record".
2. Interact with your app (e.g., trigger Rust function).
3. Stop recording and inspect timeline.
4. Look for time spent in `.wasm` frames vs JavaScript.

You can also enable **WebAssembly debugging** to see actual function names if you preserve them via `wasm-opt`.

Benchmarking Rust and JavaScript is not about proving one is superior—it's about identifying where Rust actually helps. When you approach it practically:

- Use consistent, representative data sizes.
- Minimize boundary crossings for Rust performance to shine.
- Run tests in actual browsers—not node.js—since browser engines and their Wasm JITs vary.
- Interpret results based on your application's structure, not abstract expectations.

Rust in WebAssembly is best treated as **an optimization layer** for tasks that bottleneck in JavaScript. If you apply it where it's needed, and validate it with clear benchmarks, you'll get maximum performance with minimum tradeoffs.

Chapter 7: Real-World Application Case Study

To bring everything you've learned so far into practical focus, this chapter walks you through building a complete WebAssembly-powered Rust application that runs in the browser. You'll see how to structure the project, organize your code, connect it with JavaScript, optimize for performance, and finally measure the results. The goal is not just to demonstrate what's possible, but to provide a working mental model for building maintainable, high-performance apps using Rust and Wasm in real frontend scenarios.

The example in this chapter will be a **Markdown-to-HTML converter**, implemented in Rust, compiled to WebAssembly, and integrated with a web-based UI using HTML and JavaScript.

This project is compact enough to fit in one chapter but powerful enough to show off real-world principles: text processing, DOM interaction, performance benchmarking, packaging, and frontend integration.

Building a Full Web App (Markdown Converter)

To fully understand the power and practicality of Rust and WebAssembly on the web, we're going to walk through building a complete frontend application: a Markdown converter. This app will take raw Markdown input, process it using high-performance Rust code compiled to WebAssembly, and render the result directly into a browser DOM element. You'll write code in Rust for parsing and transforming content, expose only the necessary bindings to JavaScript, and use standard web technologies to create an interactive user experience.

This section doesn't provide a toy example. It gives you a robust, browser-ready workflow with performance benefits, clear structure, and room to scale. The Markdown converter highlights one of the strongest use cases for Rust-Wasm on the frontend: **high-speed content processing without relying on JavaScript dependencies**.

Step 1: Rust Project Setup with Wasm Support

Start by creating a new Rust library crate:

```
wasm-pack new md_converter
cd md_converter
```

This scaffold sets up everything you need: lib.rs, a Cargo.toml configured for WebAssembly, and a basic example.

Update Cargo.toml

Add the dependencies and set up the release profile to optimize for binary size:

```
[dependencies]
wasm-bindgen = "0.2"
pulldown-cmark = "0.9"
wee_alloc = "0.4"

[lib]
crate-type = ["cdylib"]

[profile.release]
opt-level = "z"
lto = true
codegen-units = 1
```

- wasm-bindgen allows Rust to interoperate with JavaScript.
- pulldown-cmark is a fast, pure Rust Markdown parser.
- wee_alloc is a compact allocator that reduces .wasm binary size.

Step 2: Writing the Markdown Logic in Rust

Open src/lib.rs. First, include the necessary imports and configure the global allocator:

```
use wasm_bindgen::prelude::*;
use pulldown_cmark::{Parser, Options,
html::push_html};
use wee_alloc::WeeAlloc;

#[global_allocator]
static ALLOC: WeeAlloc = WeeAlloc::INIT;
```

Now implement the Markdown converter function that will be called from JavaScript:

```
#[wasm_bindgen]
pub fn convert_markdown(input: &str) -> String {
    let mut options = Options::empty();
    options.insert(Options::ENABLE_STRIKETHROUGH);
    options.insert(Options::ENABLE_TABLES);
    options.insert(Options::ENABLE_FOOTNOTES);
    options.insert(Options::ENABLE_TASKLISTS);

    let parser = Parser::new_ext(input, options);
    let mut html_output = String::new();
    push_html(&mut html_output, parser);
    html_output
}
```

This function takes a Markdown string, parses it using `pulldown-cmark`, and returns valid HTML. No memory pointers or unsafe code needed—just safe, idiomatic Rust.

Step 3: Building the WebAssembly Module

Build your crate for the web using `wasm-pack`:

```
wasm-pack build --release --target web
```

The output appears in the `pkg/` folder and includes:

- A `.wasm` binary
- A JavaScript wrapper module (`.js`) that can be imported in the browser

Step 4: Creating the Frontend UI

Create a file named `index.html` at the root of your project (or in a `public/` folder if using a bundler).

```
<!DOCTYPE html>
<html lang="en">
<head>
```

```html
    <meta charset="UTF-8" />
    <title>Markdown Converter (Rust + Wasm)</title>
    <style>
      body { font-family: sans-serif; padding: 20px;
}
      textarea, #output { width: 100%; height: 250px;
margin-bottom: 20px; }
      #output { border: 1px solid #ccc; padding:
10px; background: #fafafa; }
    </style>
  </head>
  <body>
    <h1>Markdown to HTML</h1>
    <textarea id="editor"># Hello, WebAssembly!\n\n-
This is parsed in Rust.</textarea>
    <button id="render">Render Markdown</button>
    <div id="output"></div>

    <script type="module">
      import init, { convert_markdown } from
"./pkg/md_converter.js";

      async function main() {
        await init();

        const editor =
document.getElementById("editor");
        const output =
document.getElementById("output");
        const button =
document.getElementById("render");

        button.addEventListener("click", () => {
          const raw = editor.value;
          const html = convert_markdown(raw);
          output.innerHTML = html;
        });
      }

      main();
    </script>
  </body>
```

```
</html>
```

This frontend consists of a Markdown input area, a render button, and a div for the output. The entire transformation is handled by your Rust-compiled WebAssembly module.

Step 5: Serving and Testing the App

To test the app in a browser, you need to serve it over HTTP (due to Wasm's loading restrictions).

Install and run a simple server:

```
npm install -g serve

serve .
```

Then open `http://localhost:3000`. Type Markdown into the textarea and click "Render Markdown." You'll see rendered HTML in real time—processed by Rust.

Step 6: Production Optimization

Before deploying, optimize your `.wasm` binary with `wasm-opt`:

```
wasm-opt -Oz --strip-debug -o
pkg/md_converter_bg.wasm pkg/md_converter_bg.wasm
```

This shrinks your binary significantly—often reducing it from 200KB+ to under 50KB (and even less when compressed with Gzip or Brotli). This matters for first-load performance and bandwidth usage.

Step 7: Extension Ideas for Real-World Use

Once the base application is working, you can extend it easily:

- Add **syntax highlighting** to code blocks using `highlight.js` in JavaScript.
- Integrate **live preview** by rendering on input change, not just button click.
- Add **export to file** (e.g., allow downloading rendered HTML).

- Use a Rust crate like `ammonia` to sanitize HTML output.
- Add a benchmarking mode to compare Rust vs JavaScript Markdown parsing.

You now have a full web application that:

- Uses Rust to parse Markdown into HTML
- Compiles to WebAssembly and runs directly in the browser
- Communicates with JavaScript via safe, minimal bindings
- Performs fast and reliably with a small, optimized binary footprint

This type of application architecture—offloading complex or performance-critical tasks to Rust, while maintaining interactivity and rendering in the frontend—is how Rust-Wasm apps are built at scale. This structure can be adapted to other workloads such as image processing, audio synthesis, data validation, or text transformation. The pattern remains the same: **Rust for compute, JS for orchestration, WebAssembly for performance portability**.

Project Structure and Module Organization

As your Rust and WebAssembly applications grow in complexity, organizing your code becomes critically important. A clear project structure ensures that your logic is easy to navigate, reusable, testable, and maintainable. Without this, small projects quickly become tangled, especially when combining Rust's strict type system, the WebAssembly compilation target, and JavaScript bindings.

This section explains how to structure a real Rust-Wasm project with multiple source files, internal modules, well-defined boundaries between JavaScript-exposed code and private Rust logic, and a clean separation of concerns. You'll see how to split your project into functional components while keeping the WebAssembly interface minimal and efficient.

The Role of Each Layer

In a typical Rust-Wasm application, you have three layers:

- **Core Logic (Pure Rust)**: Performs the real computation or data transformation. This layer does not use `wasm-bindgen`. It is purely internal and testable using standard Rust tools.

- **Interface Layer (Wasm Bindings)**: Exposes a minimal, public API to JavaScript. This is where `#[wasm_bindgen]` appears. It acts as a controlled bridge between the outside world and your Rust logic.
- **Web Assets (HTML/JS)**: The frontend (usually HTML, CSS, and JavaScript) loads the `.wasm` file and interacts with exported Rust functions.

By keeping the first two layers separate, you avoid unnecessary bindings, reduce glue code size, and improve testability.

Recommended Project Structure

Let's take the Markdown converter project and expand it into a modular format:

```
md_converter/
├── Cargo.toml
├── src/
│   ├── lib.rs              # wasm entry point
│   ├── interface.rs        # public functions exposed
to JavaScript
│   ├── parser.rs           # core markdown processing
logic
│   └── utils.rs            # helper functions and
shared logic
├── pkg/                    # wasm-pack output
└── www/
    ├── index.html
    └── main.js
```

`lib.rs`: Entry Point for wasm-pack

This file defines what should be compiled and exposed to JavaScript. It should remain minimal, delegating most work to internal modules.

```
mod interface;
mod parser;
mod utils;

pub use interface::*;
```

Here, `interface.rs` contains all `#[wasm_bindgen]` bindings. The rest of your Rust logic stays unexposed and fully testable.

`interface.rs`: Public Bindings for JavaScript

This module is the only one that uses `wasm-bindgen`. It acts as the boundary where types cross between JavaScript and Rust.

```rust
use wasm_bindgen::prelude::*;
use crate::parser::render_markdown;

#[wasm_bindgen]
pub fn convert_markdown(input: &str) -> String {
    render_markdown(input)
}
```

This function is visible to JavaScript. The rest of your logic lives in `parser.rs` and is isolated from Wasm bindings, which reduces binary bloat and makes testing easier.

`parser.rs`: Core Markdown Transformation

This module does the actual parsing and rendering. It has no knowledge of WebAssembly and no dependencies on `wasm-bindgen`.

```rust
use pulldown_cmark::{Parser, Options,
html::push_html};

pub fn render_markdown(input: &str) -> String {
    let mut options = Options::empty();
    options.insert(Options::ENABLE_STRIKETHROUGH);
    options.insert(Options::ENABLE_TABLES);
    options.insert(Options::ENABLE_FOOTNOTES);
    options.insert(Options::ENABLE_TASKLISTS);

    let parser = Parser::new_ext(input, options);
    let mut html_output = String::new();
    push_html(&mut html_output, parser);
    html_output
}
```

This code is 100% safe, idiomatic Rust. It can be tested like any other backend function without compiling to WebAssembly.

`utils.rs`: Reusable Utility Functions

This file holds logic that could be used across modules, like string manipulation, logging (if you add console output via `web_sys::console`), or buffer validation.

```rust
pub fn sanitize_input(input: &str) -> &str {
    input.trim()
}
```

You can call this inside `parser.rs` or `interface.rs`, depending on where input validation or pre-processing belongs.

JavaScript Integration (Frontend)

In `www/main.js`:

```javascript
import init, { convert_markdown } from
"../pkg/md_converter.js";

async function run() {
   await init();
   const textarea =
document.getElementById("editor");
   const output = document.getElementById("output");

   textarea.addEventListener("input", () => {
     const raw = textarea.value;
     const html = convert_markdown(raw);
     output.innerHTML = html;
   });
}

run();
```

The JavaScript layer never interacts directly with internal Rust code. It only sees `convert_markdown`, making your app easy to maintain and refactor.

Benefits of This Structure

- **Clear separation** between Wasm bindings and core logic
- **Minimal surface area** for JavaScript to call into
- **Smaller binaries** because internal Rust modules are not exported
- **Better testability**, since pure logic doesn't depend on `wasm-bindgen`
- **Scalability**, as features grow, modules can be independently developed and reasoned about

Testing Strategy

You can test all of `parser.rs` and `utils.rs` using standard Rust unit tests:

```rust
#[cfg(test)]
mod tests {
    use super::*;

    #[test]
    fn renders_basic_md() {
        let html = render_markdown("# Hello");
        assert!(html.contains("<h1>Hello</h1>"));
    }
}
```

You do **not** need to compile to Wasm for these tests. Only `interface.rs` needs to be validated in browser or through integration tests involving WebAssembly.

Good project structure is not just about cleanliness—it directly affects performance, maintainability, and productivity. By separating your Rust-Wasm project into:

- A minimal **Wasm interface layer**
- A clean **core logic layer**
- A flexible **JavaScript orchestration layer**

—you ensure that your application is lean, testable, and ready for real-world scale. This structure is suitable for anything from Markdown parsers to image processors, data visualizers, or computational frontends powered by Rust. It lets Rust focus on what it does best—safe, fast computation—while JavaScript handles the interactivity and presentation.

Packaging for Deployment

Once your Rust + WebAssembly application is complete and working in development, the final step is to package it correctly for deployment. This phase isn't just about getting the files ready for a web server—it's about optimizing them for production, organizing the output for reliability, ensuring compatibility across browsers, and applying strategies that reduce load times and bandwidth usage.

This section walks you through a professional deployment process tailored for Rust-Wasm projects. It covers how to produce a clean release build, apply binary optimizations, bundle frontend assets, serve or host your app, and configure caching and compression for performance.

Step 1: Build the Release Version

Before anything else, you need to compile your WebAssembly module using `wasm-pack` in release mode.

```
wasm-pack build --release --target web
```

This command generates the final `.wasm` file and a JavaScript glue module in the `pkg/` directory.

The `--target web` flag is important here. It tells `wasm-pack` to produce JavaScript that's compatible with native ES Modules in browsers, rather than CommonJS or bundler-specific formats like `nodejs` or `bundler`.

At this stage, your file structure should look like:

```
my_project/
├── pkg/
│    ├── my_project_bg.wasm
│    ├── my_project.js
│    └── my_project.d.ts (optional, if TypeScript is
enabled)
```

Step 2: Optimize the `.wasm` Binary

The raw `.wasm` file generated by Rust and `wasm-bindgen` is functional but not yet optimized. It contains unused metadata, debug sections, and duplicated instructions.

Use `wasm-opt` to shrink and optimize the binary:

```
wasm-opt -Oz --strip-debug --strip-producers \
  -o pkg/my_project_bg.wasm pkg/my_project_bg.wasm
```

- `-Oz`: Optimize aggressively for size (preferred for frontend).
- `--strip-debug`: Removes debug sections.
- `--strip-producers`: Removes toolchain info.

This alone can shrink your binary by 30–70%, especially when combined with `wee_alloc` and a clean release profile.

If your `.wasm` file was originally 180 KB, expect it to drop to 60 KB or lower.

Step 3: Gzip or Brotli Compression

After optimizing the binary, compress it for HTTP delivery.

Browsers expect compressed files for performance, and most CDNs serve compressed content by default. If you're self-hosting or using static site platforms (like GitHub Pages, Netlify, or Vercel), ensure your `.wasm` file is compressed.

Example using Gzip:

```
gzip -k -9 pkg/my_project_bg.wasm
```

This creates a `my_project_bg.wasm.gz` file. The `-k` flag keeps the original file, and `-9` enables maximum compression.

If your server supports Brotli (like Nginx or Cloudflare):

```
brotli -Z pkg/my_project_bg.wasm
```

You can store both `.wasm.gz` and `.wasm.br` and configure your server to choose the right one based on the browser's `Accept-Encoding` header.

Step 4: Organizing Final Assets

Create a `dist/` folder (or `public/`, `build/`, etc.) and organize the deployable files:

```
dist/
├── index.html
├── main.js
├── pkg/
│       ├── my_project.js
│       ├── my_project_bg.wasm
│       ├── my_project_bg.wasm.gz (optional)
│       └── my_project.d.ts
```

Place your static files—HTML, CSS, JS, and the `pkg/` folder—inside this directory. This makes deployment and routing simpler and ensures everything is in one place.

Step 5: Hosting the WebAssembly App

You can deploy the `dist/` folder to any static hosting service:

Local testing with `serve`:

```
npm install -g serve

serve dist
```

GitHub Pages:

Push the `dist/` folder to the `gh-pages` branch and enable Pages in your repository settings.

```
npx gh-pages -d dist
```

Netlify:

Drag and drop the `dist/` folder into Netlify's UI or connect it to your Git repo.

Vercel:

Use the `vercel` CLI or Git integration. It supports ES modules and `.wasm` out of the box.

Step 6: Configuring the Server (Headers and Caching)

If you're running your own server (e.g., Nginx), add appropriate headers for **.wasm**:

```
location ~* \.wasm$ {
    add_header Content-Type application/wasm;
    add_header Cache-Control "public, max-
age=31536000, immutable";
    gzip_static on;   # Serve pre-gzipped file
}
```

Use `Cache-Control:  immutable` for versioned `.wasm` files to allow aggressive caching.

Also ensure you serve the JS loader file (`my_project.js`) with `Content-Type: application/javascript` and allow CORS if you're hosting assets on a CDN.

Step 7: Versioning and Cache Busting

To avoid stale caches when updating your app:

- Use unique file names (e.g., `my_project_bg.abc123.wasm`) with content hashes.
- Update the HTML and JS references accordingly.
- In CI/CD, use a build script that fingerprints the `.wasm` and `.js` files.

This is especially important if you host through CDNs or expect clients to cache aggressively.

Packaging your Rust + Wasm app for deployment involves more than building the binary. To prepare for production:

- Build in release mode with proper compiler flags.
- Optimize the `.wasm` using `wasm-opt`.

- Compress assets using Gzip or Brotli.
- Organize your output into a deployable `dist/` structure.
- Use static hosting or a CDN to deliver your app efficiently.
- Set correct headers, MIME types, and caching policies.

These steps ensure that your application doesn't just work—it loads quickly, uses minimal bandwidth, and remains fast and reliable across devices and network conditions. A well-packaged Wasm app reflects the same discipline and polish as the Rust code behind it.

Comparing Performance Gains

One of the strongest motivations for using Rust with WebAssembly in web applications is performance. Rust is designed to be fast, predictable, and safe without relying on garbage collection. When compiled to WebAssembly, Rust brings its performance benefits directly to the browser, often outperforming equivalent JavaScript code—especially in CPU-intensive or allocation-heavy workloads.

But claims of performance need to be validated. Real-world benchmarks show where Rust-Wasm provides real gains, and where its benefits are negligible or even counterproductive. This section focuses on practical techniques to **measure, compare, and interpret** performance across Rust and JavaScript implementations using meaningful tasks and consistent testing.

Choosing What to Measure

Before comparing performance, be clear about the scope. Focus on operations where:

- The workload is **CPU-bound**, not dominated by DOM updates.
- Data structures are **numeric or binary**, not deeply nested JavaScript objects.
- The function is **self-contained** and can run repeatedly with measurable cost.
- The **Rust function replaces or supplements** a real JavaScript alternative.

In our case study, we're comparing a **Markdown-to-HTML converter** written in Rust using `pulldown-cmark` with a common JavaScript implementation using `marked`.

Setting Up a Controlled Benchmark

Let's define both implementations clearly so we're measuring the same thing.

JavaScript Implementation (`marked.js`)

Include this in your HTML:

```
<script
src="https://cdn.jsdelivr.net/npm/marked/marked.min
.js"></script>
```

Define a function:

```
function renderMarkdownJS(input) {

    return marked.parse(input);

}
```

Rust Implementation (`lib.rs`)

```
use wasm_bindgen::prelude::*;
use pulldown_cmark::{Parser, Options,
html::push_html};

#[wasm_bindgen]
pub fn render_markdown(input: &str) -> String {
    let mut options = Options::all();
    let parser = Parser::new_ext(input, options);
    let mut html_output = String::new();
    push_html(&mut html_output, parser);
    html_output
}
```

Compile using:

```
wasm-pack build --release --target web
```

Benchmarking in the Browser

Use `console.time()` for real-time browser benchmarks.

```javascript
import init, { render_markdown } from
"./pkg/md_converter.js";

async function runBenchmarks() {
  await init();

  const input = `# Markdown Benchmark

  This is a test paragraph.

  - Bullet point 1
  - Bullet point 2
  - Bullet point 3

  \`\`\`rust
  fn main() {
    println!("Hello, world!");
  }
  \`\`\`

  `.repeat(200); // ~15 KB Markdown

  console.time("JavaScript");
  const htmlJS = renderMarkdownJS(input);
  console.timeEnd("JavaScript");

  console.time("Rust/Wasm");
  const htmlRust = render_markdown(input);
  console.timeEnd("Rust/Wasm");
}
```

Sample Output:

```
JavaScript: 65.7ms

Rust/Wasm: 34.2ms
```

This clearly shows that for large Markdown documents, the Rust implementation is nearly twice as fast.

Real-World Performance Considerations

Performance gains from Rust-Wasm are most noticeable when:

- The workload involves tight loops, like hashing, encoding, or parsing.
- Data sizes grow (e.g., 10K+ lines of Markdown or text).
- You batch the data into fewer calls (crossing the JS-Wasm boundary is expensive).

Performance may be equivalent or worse when:

- The task is dominated by JavaScript-native APIs like DOM manipulation.
- The function is too short—boundary cost can outweigh computation cost.
- You make many small interop calls (e.g., 100,000 tiny Rust invocations).

General principle: Run *more* work per call from JavaScript into Rust to maximize throughput.

Measuring Memory Use

Besides speed, WebAssembly can improve memory characteristics:

- **No garbage collection pauses** like in JavaScript.
- **Deterministic allocation and release** via RAII patterns.
- **Compact memory footprint** when using crates like `wee_alloc`.

To monitor memory:

1. Open DevTools > Performance > Memory tab.
2. Trigger both versions repeatedly.
3. Observe heap growth over time.

Rust-Wasm should use less memory for equivalent work, particularly under sustained load.

Optional: Profiling with DevTools

For deeper analysis:

1. Open the **Performance tab** in Chrome.

2. Click "Record", then run both render functions.
3. Stop recording.
4. Analyze the flame graph to compare time spent in Wasm vs JavaScript.

Use `wasm-opt` during your build to remove unnecessary instructions:

```
wasm-opt -Oz -o pkg/md_converter_bg.wasm
pkg/md_converter_bg.wasm
```

You'll see a tighter, faster binary as a result.

Rust-Wasm delivers measurable performance improvements in frontend applications, especially when:

- Processing large, structured, or repetitive data (like Markdown)
- Offloading computation-heavy tasks from JavaScript
- Minimizing interop and batching input

By testing in real browsers, using meaningful input sizes, and comparing against well-known JS libraries, you get hard evidence of how much performance Rust adds. Not every function needs to be moved to Wasm, but for the ones that do, the gains can be significant—and quantifiable.

Chapter 8: Testing and Debugging Rust-Wasm Code

Writing WebAssembly applications in Rust means you inherit Rust's strong guarantees for correctness, safety, and performance. But it also introduces new challenges: you're working across a boundary between two languages (Rust and JavaScript), deploying to a browser, and targeting a compact binary format that lacks many of the debugging luxuries developers rely on in native development.

Unit Testing with `wasm-bindgen-test`

When developing applications with Rust compiled to WebAssembly, you still benefit from Rust's robust testing ecosystem—but you'll need a few additional tools when running tests in the browser or a JavaScript runtime. The standard `cargo test` isn't compatible with WebAssembly targets. Instead, the Rust-Wasm ecosystem provides a tool called `wasm-bindgen-test` that allows you to write and execute unit tests in a real Wasm runtime environment (either headless in Node.js or in a real browser).

The goal of unit testing is to validate logic in isolation. In Rust-Wasm applications, logic often involves input/output to JavaScript, string manipulation, data transformation, and interactions with browser-like data. Standard Rust tests won't work here because `wasm32-unknown-unknown` targets can't execute using `cargo test`.

`wasm-bindgen-test` bridges this gap by compiling your tests to Wasm, wrapping them in JavaScript, and executing them in a JS engine such as Chrome, Firefox, or Node.js. This lets you validate your logic **exactly as it will run in production**.

Step 1: Add `wasm-bindgen-test` to Your Project

First, update your `Cargo.toml` to include `wasm-bindgen-test` under `[dev-dependencies]`:

```
[dev-dependencies]
wasm-bindgen-test = "0.3"
```

```
[lib]
crate-type = ["cdylib", "rlib"]
```

Set `cdylib` so that wasm-pack can generate a binary, and `rlib` so tests can be linked internally.

Step 2: Configure Your Test Environment

In your test file (or `lib.rs` if you're embedding tests), configure wasm-bindgen-test to run in the browser or Node.js:

```
#[cfg(test)]
use wasm_bindgen_test::wasm_bindgen_test_configure;

#[cfg(test)]
wasm_bindgen_test_configure!(run_in_browser);
```

You can also configure `run_in_node` if your logic does not rely on browser APIs like DOM access.

Then import the macro:

```
#[cfg(test)]

use wasm_bindgen_test::*;
```

Step 3: Writing a Simple Test

Let's write a function and test it.

Code to test (e.g., `src/utils.rs`):

```
pub fn reverse(input: &str) -> String {
    input.chars().rev().collect()
}
```

Test module:

```
#[cfg(test)]
mod tests {
    use super::*;
    use wasm_bindgen_test::*;
```

```
    wasm_bindgen_test_configure!(run_in_browser);

    #[wasm_bindgen_test]
    fn reverses_strings_correctly() {
        let result = reverse("Rust");
        assert_eq!(result, "tsuR");
    }

    #[wasm_bindgen_test]
    fn handles_unicode() {
        let result = reverse("👨‍👩‍👧");
        assert_eq!(result, "👧👩‍👨👨"); // This will
fail if grapheme clusters aren't handled
    }
}
```

Run your test suite:

```
wasm-pack test --headless --firefox
```

Or in Chrome:

```
wasm-pack test --headless --chrome
```

For simpler testing (non-DOM environments), use Node.js:

```
wasm-pack test --node
```

This compiles your test code to Wasm and runs it in the selected engine, giving full test output in the terminal.

Step 4: Asserting on Wasm-Compatible Types

You can test functions returning String, bool, integers, floats, or anything that stays within the safe boundaries of what wasm-bindgen can translate across.

For example, if you expose a function like:

```
#[wasm_bindgen]
```

```rust
pub fn add(a: i32, b: i32) -> i32 {
    a + b
}
```

You can still test it internally using:

```rust
#[wasm_bindgen_test]
fn test_addition() {
    assert_eq!(add(3, 2), 5);
}
```

Avoid testing functions that deal with JsValue, web_sys::Element, or other interop-heavy types directly unless you're writing integration tests—unit tests should isolate pure logic where possible.

Step 5: Testing Failing Cases and Panics

You can test error-handling behavior too:

```rust
pub fn safe_divide(a: i32, b: i32) -> Result<i32,
&'static str> {
    if b == 0 {
        Err("division by zero")
    } else {
        Ok(a / b)
    }
}
#[wasm_bindgen_test]
fn handles_division_by_zero() {
    let result = safe_divide(10, 0);
    assert!(result.is_err());
    assert_eq!(result.unwrap_err(), "division by
zero");
}
```

This approach encourages error-safe code and protects against silent failures at the WebAssembly boundary.

Step 6: Organizing Your Test Modules

Structure your test files to match your module layout. For example:

133

```
src/
├── lib.rs
├── parser.rs
├── utils.rs
tests/
└── integration.rs
```

You can place internal unit tests within each module (`parser.rs`, `utils.rs`) and have a dedicated `tests/integration.rs` file for end-to-end or interop tests.

Keep in mind that `wasm-pack test` only runs tests inside the crate (not in the outer `tests/` directory) unless you're using a custom test harness.

Best Practices

- **Avoid over-exporting.** Test internal functions directly, not through `#[wasm_bindgen]` wrappers.
- **Use test-specific data.** Avoid running full Markdown parsers on static files—test small, meaningful samples.
- **Keep unit tests in Rust.** Reserve JavaScript tests (Jest, Mocha, etc.) for integration tests.
- **Write fast, isolated tests.** Slow Wasm tests break CI/CD cycles.

Using `wasm-bindgen-test` allows you to keep your testing entirely in Rust, even for Wasm-targeted code. You maintain correctness, confidence, and speed by:

- Compiling tests to Wasm and running them in real browsers or JS engines
- Testing logic exactly as it will run in production
- Catching regressions early, before deployment
- Ensuring behavior across JavaScript boundaries is predictable and safe

This keeps your codebase stable and your Rust-Wasm integration clean, testable, and production-ready.

Debugging Rust in the Browser

When developing Rust applications that compile to WebAssembly, debugging can feel unfamiliar at first. Instead of working directly with Rust code in a terminal or an IDE, you're deploying to a browser environment with its own debugging tools, runtime behavior, and limitations. But thanks to improving browser support and careful tooling within the Rust-Wasm ecosystem, it's entirely possible to inspect, log, and step through your Rust logic—even inside WebAssembly binaries—using modern development practices.

WebAssembly is a low-level, binary format. When you compile Rust to Wasm in release mode, the result is highly optimized machine code with minimal debugging metadata. To debug effectively, you need to:

1. **Compile with debug symbols enabled**
2. **Use a browser that supports Wasm source mapping**
3. **Expose logs and errors to the JavaScript console**
4. **Place meaningful breakpoints and step through code**

Let's go through these steps using a real example.

Step 1: Build with Debug Information

By default, release builds strip debug symbols for size. When debugging, **don't use `--release`**. Instead, build your Wasm package using:

```
wasm-pack build --target web --dev
```

This retains debug symbols in the generated `.wasm` file and skips aggressive optimizations that would otherwise inline or obscure your code.

If you're building manually (outside of wasm-pack), set the following in `Cargo.toml`:

```
[profile.dev]

opt-level = 0

debug = true
```

This ensures human-readable names and valid source mapping sections.

Step 2: Use Browser DevTools to Inspect Wasm

Once your `.wasm` is loaded in a browser, open the **Developer Tools** in Chrome, Firefox, or Edge.

In **Chrome**:

1. Go to the **Sources** tab.
2. In the left sidebar, expand WASM → your module.
3. You'll see raw .wat (WebAssembly Text) or even partially reconstructed Rust source if debug symbols are intact.
4. Click on a function to inspect or set breakpoints.

In **Firefox**:

1. Open DevTools → **Debugger**
2. WebAssembly frames appear under the **Sources** panel when Wasm is loaded.
3. Firefox may label these as (wasm) or by module name.

You can step through instructions, view function calls, and inspect the call stack—even across JavaScript → Rust boundaries.

Step 3: Use Console Logging Inside Rust

To debug dynamically at runtime, print internal values from Rust using the browser's console.

Add web-sys to your dependencies:

```
[dependencies]
web-sys = { version = "0.3", features = ["console"]
}
```

Then define a logging helper:

```
use web_sys::console;

pub fn log(msg: &str) {
    console::log_1(&msg.into());
}
```

Use it anywhere in your code:

```
log("Starting markdown render...");

log(&format!("Input length: {}", input.len()));
```

This outputs to the browser's console like a standard `console.log()` call.

Step 4: Enable Panic Messages in the Browser

Rust panics are normally silent in Wasm unless you explicitly hook them. To get stack traces and panic messages printed to the console, use the `console_error_panic_hook` crate.

Add to `Cargo.toml`:

```toml
[dependencies]
console_error_panic_hook = "0.1"
```

And initialize it once at startup:

```rust
use console_error_panic_hook;

#[wasm_bindgen(start)]
pub fn main() {
    console_error_panic_hook::set_once();
    log("Rust-Wasm module initialized.");
}
```

Now when something like this occurs:

```rust
panic!("Something went wrong");
```

…you'll see a detailed error in the browser console, including the line number and call stack if debug symbols are present.

Step 5: Example: Debugging a Faulty Markdown Parser

Let's say you wrote the following Rust function:

```rust
pub fn extract_title(md: &str) -> &str {
    md.lines()
        .find(|line| line.starts_with("# "))
        .expect("Markdown title not found")
        .trim_start_matches("# ")
}
```

If a user provides input without a # title, it panics.

You can make this safer and easier to debug:

```
pub fn extract_title(md: &str) -> Option<String> {
    for line in md.lines() {
        log(&format!("Checking line: {}", line));
        if line.starts_with("# ") {
            let title = line.trim_start_matches("#
").to_string();
            log(&format!("Found title: {}",
title));
            return Some(title);
        }
    }
    log("No title found.");
    None
}
```

This turns runtime panics into controlled logs, visible immediately in the browser console.

Step 6: Using Source Maps (Optional Advanced Setup)

If you want to **see original Rust line numbers in browser stack traces**, you can generate source maps using `wasm-sourcemap`:

```
cargo install wasm-sourcemap

wasm-sourcemap generate -w pkg/my_project_bg.wasm -
o pkg/my_project_bg.wasm.map
```

Then serve both the `.wasm` file and its `.wasm.map` in production with:

```
Content-Type: application/wasm
SourceMap: /pkg/my_project_bg.wasm.map
```

Note: This is still experimental and has varying support across browsers. It's most helpful in larger apps or teams with CI diagnostics.

Step 7: Debugging JavaScript ↔ Rust Interop

Sometimes the problem is not in Rust directly, but in how JavaScript interacts with Rust-Wasm.

Example issue:

```
#[wasm_bindgen]
pub fn repeat(input: &str, count: usize) -> String
{
    input.repeat(count)
}
```

And in JS:

```
repeat("hello", "3"); // Passing string instead of
number
```

This throws an error, but it might not be obvious. To catch it more gracefully:

```
#[wasm_bindgen]
pub fn repeat_checked(input: &str, count: JsValue)
-> Result<String, JsValue> {
    let count = count.as_f64().ok_or_else(||
JsValue::from_str("Invalid count"))?;
    Ok(input.repeat(count as usize))
}
```

This pattern protects your Rust from unsafe or unexpected JS input, while producing cleaner errors in the browser console.

Debugging Rust-Wasm in the browser is fully achievable with the right tools and habits:

- **Build in dev mode** to retain debug symbols.
- **Use browser DevTools** to inspect Wasm functions and step through them.
- **Log from Rust** using web_sys::console.
- **Handle panics visibly** with console_error_panic_hook.
- **Validate inputs and errors** across the JS-Wasm boundary.
- **Use source maps** for deeper stack visibility when necessary.

With these strategies, you're not guessing or working blindly—you're observing your compiled Rust code live in the browser, with meaningful visibility and full confidence in your debugging process.

Logging, Error Handling, and Diagnostics

When building Rust applications for WebAssembly, your compiled .wasm code runs in a foreign environment—the browser or a JavaScript runtime like Node.js. This introduces a few challenges that aren't present in typical Rust backends. You no longer have access to `println!()` output in the terminal, panics may not show up unless explicitly handled, and debugging must be routed through tools and APIs native to the JavaScript environment.

To write resilient, observable WebAssembly applications in Rust, you need three key practices in place:

1. Structured logging from Rust to the browser console
2. Proper error propagation from Rust to JavaScript
3. Support for panic diagnostics and traceable runtime failures

Logging from Rust to the Browser Console

Rust's `println!()` does nothing in a WebAssembly context unless you manually wire it up. Instead, use the `web_sys::console` API to send logs directly to the browser's developer console.

Step 1: Add web-sys to your dependencies

```
[dependencies]
web-sys = { version = "0.3", features = ["console"]
}
```

The "console" feature enables access to `console.log`, `console.warn`, and others.

Step 2: Define log functions in Rust

```
use web_sys::console;

pub fn log(msg: &str) {
    console::log_1(&msg.into());
```

```
}

pub fn warn(msg: &str) {
    console::warn_1(&msg.into());
}

pub fn error(msg: &str) {
    console::error_1(&msg.into());
}
```

Step 3: Use in your Rust code

```
log("Starting Markdown conversion...");

warn("Received unexpected input.");

error("Failed to process content block.");
```

Each of these prints to the browser's console using its native severity levels. You can inspect the logs directly in Chrome/Firefox DevTools under the **Console** tab.

Capturing and Displaying Panics

By default, Rust panics in Wasm are silent—no error message, no stack trace, just a blank failure. To turn panics into observable browser errors, use the `console_error_panic_hook` crate.

Step 1: Add the panic hook crate

```
[dependencies]

console_error_panic_hook = "0.1"
```

Step 2: Set the hook at runtime

You can do this inside your `#[wasm_bindgen(start)]` function or early in your application:

```
use console_error_panic_hook;

#[wasm_bindgen(start)]
```

```
pub fn main() {
    console_error_panic_hook::set_once();
    log("Application started");
}
```

Step 3: Panic for testing

```
pub fn risky_operation() {

    panic!("Something went wrong!");

}
```

The message "Something went wrong!" will now appear in the browser's developer console, along with a stack trace pointing to the specific line in Rust if debug symbols are preserved (--dev build).

Handling Errors Across the JS–Rust Boundary

When you export functions from Rust to JavaScript via #[wasm_bindgen], those functions are expected to succeed. If they panic or fail without returning a Result, they can crash the WebAssembly runtime or silently fail. To handle this safely, always use Result<T, JsValue> for fallible operations.

A safe Rust function:

```
use wasm_bindgen::prelude::*;

#[wasm_bindgen]
pub fn parse_json(input: &str) -> Result<JsValue,
JsValue> {

serde_json::from_str::<serde_json::Value>(input)
        .map(JsValue::from_serde)
        .map_err(|e|
JsValue::from_str(&format!("Failed to parse JSON:
{}", e)))?
}
```

This function handles invalid input gracefully and communicates failure back to JavaScript in a structured way.

In JavaScript:

```
try {
  const value = parse_json("{ invalid json }");
  console.log("Parsed JSON:", value);
} catch (e) {
  console.error("Rust threw:", e);
}
```

This avoids hard crashes and makes it easy to debug user input errors, application bugs, and boundary violations.

Enhancing Diagnostics with Type Safety and Descriptions

When you design Rust functions for WebAssembly, every exposed function should either:

- Be infallible, or
- Return a `Result` with an informative `Err` message

Avoid panicking in exported functions unless you're prototyping. Instead, prefer structured errors with clear semantics.

Example: Validate Markdown before parsing

```
#[wasm_bindgen]
pub fn validate_and_render(input: &str) ->
Result<String, JsValue> {
    if input.trim().is_empty() {
        return Err(JsValue::from_str("Input is
empty"));
    }

    let html = render_markdown(input); // some
internal function
    Ok(html)
}
```

And in JS:

```
try {
  const html = validate_and_render(userInput);
```

```
    document.getElementById("output").innerHTML =
html;
} catch (e) {
    alert("Error: " + e.message);
}
```

This pattern enforces predictable control flow and gives users feedback without crashing the page or breaking your WebAssembly runtime.

Capturing Stack Traces and Internal State

For deeper debugging (especially in larger applications), you can emit stack traces directly in logs:

```
pub fn log_backtrace(label: &str) {
    use backtrace::Backtrace;
    let bt = Backtrace::new();
    log(&format!("{}:\n{:?}", label, bt));
}
```

This requires the `backtrace` crate:

```
[dependencies]

backtrace = "0.3"
```

Note: This is mostly useful during development. On the web, you'll want to compile with debug symbols and avoid enabling full backtraces in production due to size and performance concerns.

Common Pitfalls and How to Avoid Them

Issue	Cause	Fix
Silent crash or empty output	Panic without a hook	Use `console_error_panic_hook` and return `Result<T, JsValue>`
No logs in browser console	Used `println!()` instead of `web_sys::console::log`	Use `log()` wrappers from `web-sys`

Issue	Cause	Fix
JavaScript `undefined` from Rust	Rust panicked or returned an unwrapped `Err`	Handle errors properly in Rust with `Result<T, JsValue>`
Loss of error context	Just returned a string	Format errors with context using `format!()` or structured values
Stack trace doesn't show file/line	Compiled in `--release` mode or stripped debug info	Use `--dev` build for debugging or retain debug info manually

For any serious Rust-Wasm application, robust logging and error diagnostics are essential. The moment you hand your code over to the browser, you lose the familiar Rust CLI output and need to replace it with structured, observable behavior:

- Use `web-sys::console` to emit logs into the browser.
- Use `console_error_panic_hook` to capture and display panics clearly.
- Always return `Result<T, JsValue>` for fallible functions exported to JavaScript.
- Use descriptive, structured errors with context and stack trace information where applicable.
- Avoid relying on panics for control flow—treat your WebAssembly surface like a public API.

With these practices, your Rust code behaves predictably and visibly inside the browser, making your application easier to test, debug, and maintain.

Interoperability Test Strategies

When working with Rust and WebAssembly, your code doesn't run in isolation—it runs as part of a larger application that often depends on interaction between Rust and JavaScript. Whether you're calling Rust functions from JavaScript or using Rust to manipulate browser APIs, you need to ensure this interaction is reliable, correct, and testable.

Interoperability bugs are particularly difficult to spot because they occur at the boundary where two ecosystems meet. A Rust function may work perfectly on its own. A JavaScript snippet may look valid. But when combined, mismatched types, incorrect assumptions, or subtle conversion issues can cause runtime errors or unexpected behavior.

To catch these problems early, you need clear interoperability test strategies. In this section, you'll learn how to validate the correctness and resilience of your Rust-JavaScript interface through focused, maintainable, and automated testing approaches.

Purpose of Interoperability Tests

Interoperability tests check that:

- Data passed from JavaScript to Rust is interpreted correctly in Rust.
- Values returned from Rust to JavaScript maintain their expected shape and semantics.
- JavaScript handles errors and exceptions thrown or returned by Rust functions.
- Complex data structures like arrays, maps, and custom objects cross the Wasm boundary safely and predictably.
- Event handlers or callbacks wired across the boundary behave as expected.

These tests are crucial when you expose Rust code to a browser-based UI, a JavaScript framework, or external APIs.

Strategy 1: Use `wasm-bindgen`'s Type Compatibility in Unit Tests

For functions that accept or return only basic types (`String`, `i32`, `f64`, `bool`, `Vec<u8>`, etc.), you can write regular Rust unit tests to simulate JavaScript input.

Example: Rust-side test with a simulated JS-like input

```rust
#[wasm_bindgen]
pub fn double(x: i32) -> i32 {
    x * 2
}
```

In Rust:

```rust
#[cfg(test)]
```

```
mod tests {
    use super::*;
    use wasm_bindgen_test::*;

    #[wasm_bindgen_test]
    fn doubles_integer_values() {
        assert_eq!(double(4), 8);
    }
}
```

This confirms that JavaScript's `number` → Rust's `i32` conversion works cleanly.

Strategy 2: Use JavaScript Tests to Validate Wasm Exports

For full interoperability validation, write JavaScript (or TypeScript) tests that directly invoke Rust-Wasm exports and assert on the result.

You can use test frameworks like **Jest**, **Vitest**, or **Mocha** for this.

Example setup using Jest

Build your crate:

```
wasm-pack build --target web
```

Create a test file (`interop.test.js`):

```
import init, { double } from
"../pkg/your_crate.js";

beforeAll(async () => {
await init();
});

test("doubles input correctly", () => {
expect(double(10)).toBe(20);
});
```

Run the tests:

```
npx jest
```

This verifies that your compiled Wasm exports are callable and behave correctly when invoked with actual JavaScript types.

Strategy 3: Test Structured Data Round-Trip

Passing complex data like arrays or objects between JavaScript and Rust requires correct serialization and deserialization. `wasm-bindgen` provides some built-in conversion, but you often need to work with `JsValue` or use `serde`.

Example: Accepting JSON from JavaScript

Rust function:

```
use wasm_bindgen::prelude::*;
use serde::{Deserialize, Serialize};
use serde_wasm_bindgen;

#[derive(Serialize, Deserialize)]
pub struct User {
    name: String,
    age: u32,
}

#[wasm_bindgen]
pub fn greet_user(data: JsValue) -> Result<JsValue,
JsValue> {
    let user: User =
serde_wasm_bindgen::from_value(data)?;
    let greeting = format!("Hello, {}! You are {}
years old.", user.name, user.age);
    Ok(JsValue::from_str(&greeting))
}
```

Test in JavaScript:

```
test("greets user with structured input", async ()
=> {
  const input = { name: "Alice", age: 30 };
  const result = greet_user(input);
  expect(result).toBe("Hello, Alice! You are 30
years old.");
```

```
});
```

This test ensures that your serialization logic, data shape assumptions, and return formatting are all correct.

Strategy 4: Validate Error Propagation

Rust functions that return `Result<T, JsValue>` translate neatly into JavaScript exceptions. You should test both success and failure cases.

Rust:

```
#[wasm_bindgen]
pub fn divide(a: f64, b: f64) -> Result<f64,
JsValue> {
    if b == 0.0 {
        Err(JsValue::from_str("Division by zero"))
    } else {
        Ok(a / b)
    }
}
```

JavaScript test:

```
test("handles division errors", () => {
  expect(() => divide(10, 0)).toThrow("Division by
zero");
});

test("returns result for valid input", () => {
  expect(divide(10, 2)).toBe(5);
});
```

You now have coverage for both correct paths and boundary failures.

Strategy 5: Event Handler and Callback Testing

If you expose Rust functions that JavaScript registers as event handlers or vice versa, you should simulate these in browser tests or headless DOM environments.

Example in Rust:

```
#[wasm_bindgen]
pub fn call_callback(cb: &js_sys::Function) ->
Result<(), JsValue> {
    cb.call0(&JsValue::NULL)?;
    Ok(())
}
```

Test in JS:

```
test("executes JS callback from Rust", () => {
  let called = false;
  const callback = () => { called = true };
  call_callback(callback);
  expect(called).toBe(true);
});
```

This test ensures the JavaScript function is callable from Rust and executes as expected.

Strategy 6: Use `wasm-bindgen-test` for Browser-Based Integration

If your function interacts with browser APIs (like DOM elements or window events), use `wasm-bindgen-test` configured to run in a real browser.

Rust:

```
#[wasm_bindgen_test]
fn test_access_dom_element() {
    use web_sys::window;
    let document =
window().unwrap().document().unwrap();
    let body = document.body().unwrap();
    assert!(body.text_content().is_some());
}
```

Run:

```
wasm-pack test --firefox --headless
```

This simulates a full browser execution and validates DOM access inside Rust-Wasm.

Interoperability testing ensures that your Rust-Wasm interface behaves consistently and safely across boundaries. To achieve full coverage:

- Test Rust functions in isolation using `wasm-bindgen-test`
- Use JavaScript test suites to exercise Rust-Wasm from the JS perspective
- Validate structured data using `serde_wasm_bindgen`
- Test error propagation to verify robust failure handling
- Cover event/callback logic to ensure interactivity is correct
- Run tests in browsers when working with DOM or native APIs

These strategies reduce regressions, catch integration bugs early, and give you complete confidence in your Rust-Wasm interface—whether you're building frontend tools, UI logic, or performance-critical browser features.

Chapter 9: Deploying Rust-Wasm to Production

Building a WebAssembly application in Rust is only half the job. Once the application is ready, you need to package it correctly, deploy it securely, and ensure that your users can load and run it efficiently from any device or network condition. This chapter walks you through the complete deployment lifecycle for Rust-Wasm applications—from packaging as npm modules to choosing hosting options, optimizing load and cache behavior, and automating deployments with CI/CD pipelines.

Packaging as npm Modules

If you want to distribute your Rust-based WebAssembly code so that it can be reused in JavaScript or TypeScript projects, packaging it as an npm module is the standard and most effective method. This allows frontend teams, Node.js developers, or build tools to integrate your Wasm functionality just like any other JavaScript library—using `import`, respecting versioning, and managing it via `package.json`.

Prerequisites

Before you begin, ensure that you have the following installed:

- Rust
- `wasm-pack`
- Node.js and npm (comes with Node)
- An npm account (create one at npmjs.com)

Install `wasm-pack` if you haven't already:

```
cargo install wasm-pack
```

This tool compiles Rust to WebAssembly, generates the JavaScript bindings, and prepares a publishable npm package.

Step 1: Create a Rust Project

Start with a new Rust library crate. If you're starting from scratch:

```
wasm-pack new rust-wasm-math

cd rust-wasm-math
```

This creates a minimal project with `src/lib.rs`, `Cargo.toml`, and the correct build configuration.

Step 2: Write Your Wasm-Exported Rust Functions

In `src/lib.rs`, define functions that you want to expose to JavaScript using `#[wasm_bindgen]`:

```rust
use wasm_bindgen::prelude::*;

// This function will be exposed to JavaScript
#[wasm_bindgen]
pub fn add(a: i32, b: i32) -> i32 {
    a + b
}

#[wasm_bindgen]
pub fn factorial(n: u32) -> u64 {
    (1..=n as u64).product()
}
```

Add this to your `Cargo.toml` to enable WebAssembly output:

```toml
[lib]

crate-type = ["cdylib"]



[dependencies]

wasm-bindgen = "0.2"
```

Make sure your crate doesn't use any standard I/O operations like `println!()` unless you're using a compatible logging setup.

Step 3: Build the Package for npm

Use `wasm-pack` to build your crate targeting the npm bundler ecosystem:

```
wasm-pack build --target bundler
```

This creates a `pkg/` folder with:

- A `.wasm` binary (`rust_wasm_math_bg.wasm`)
- A JavaScript module wrapper (`rust_wasm_math.js`)
- TypeScript declarations (`.d.ts`)
- A ready-to-publish `package.json`

This `pkg/` directory is now your npm module.

Step 4: Inspect and Customize `package.json`

Open `pkg/package.json`. You'll see entries like:

```
{
  "name": "rust-wasm-math",
  "version": "0.1.0",
  "files": [
    "rust_wasm_math_bg.wasm",
    "rust_wasm_math.js",
    "rust_wasm_math.d.ts"
  ],
  "main": "rust_wasm_math.js",
  "types": "rust_wasm_math.d.ts",
  "sideEffects": false
}
```

Make any edits here **before** publishing:

- Ensure the `name` is unique across npm.
- Add `"repository"`, `"description"`, and `"license"` fields as needed.
- Add `"module"`: `"rust_wasm_math.js"` if you're targeting modern bundlers.

Optional but recommended:

```
npm init -y  # if you want to manage versioning and
metadata manually
```

Step 5: Publish to npm

If this is your first time publishing to npm:

npm login

Then from the `pkg/` directory:

npm publish --access public

Your Rust-Wasm library is now available for global installation via:

npm install rust-wasm-math

If you're publishing to a private registry or scope (e.g., `@yourorg/rust-wasm-math`), adjust the `name` and `access` settings accordingly.

Step 6: Use in a JavaScript or TypeScript Project

After installing the npm module, use it in your frontend or Node.js application.

In JavaScript:

```
import init, { add, factorial } from 'rust-wasm-
math';

async function run() {
   await init(); // Initializes the Wasm module
   console.log("2 + 3 =", add(2, 3));
   console.log("Factorial of 5 =", factorial(5));
}

run();
```

The call to `init()` is required because it loads and instantiates the underlying WebAssembly binary asynchronously.

In TypeScript:

Type declarations are generated automatically:

```
import init, { add, factorial } from 'rust-wasm-
math';

await init();

const result: number = add(10, 5);
```

You get full autocompletion and type checking out of the box.

Step 7: Automate with CI/CD (Optional)

You can automate packaging and publishing with GitHub Actions or any CI platform.

Here's a simple `npm-publish.yml` workflow:

```
name: Publish to npm

on:
  push:
    tags:
      - 'v*.*.*'

jobs:
  publish:
    runs-on: ubuntu-latest
    steps:
      - uses: actions/checkout@v3

      - name: Install Rust
        uses: actions-rs/toolchain@v1
        with:
          toolchain: stable

      - name: Install wasm-pack
        run: cargo install wasm-pack

      - name: Build wasm
        run: wasm-pack build --target bundler
```

```
- name: Publish
  working-directory: pkg
  run: npm publish --access public
  env:
    NODE_AUTH_TOKEN: ${{ secrets.NPM_TOKEN }}
```

Add your NPM_TOKEN as a secret in your GitHub repository settings.

Publishing your Rust-Wasm crate as an npm module allows you to:

- Distribute WebAssembly-powered logic to JavaScript and TypeScript projects
- Make your logic reusable, testable, and shareable through a standard package manager
- Fully integrate with existing frontend tooling, CI/CD pipelines, and modern web development workflows

Whether you're building a high-performance parser, a utility library, or a full application module, packaging it for npm ensures compatibility and discoverability across the JavaScript ecosystem.

Hosting Options (Static Site, CDN, Serverless)

Once you've built and tested your Rust application compiled to WebAssembly, the next step is getting it into the hands of users. This means hosting it somewhere reliable, fast, and easy to maintain. Depending on your project's scope, your hosting strategy might include serving static files directly, using a content delivery network (CDN) to cache and distribute your .wasm binary, or running WebAssembly in a serverless execution environment for edge-side computation.

Each method serves a different kind of deployment need, and understanding the tradeoffs helps you choose the right one for your application.

Static Site Hosting

This is the most common and straightforward option for deploying a frontend application that uses Rust-Wasm. You simply serve a set of static assets: HTML, JavaScript, CSS, and .wasm.

What You Need

- Your compiled Wasm package (`pkg/` from `wasm-pack build`)
- A single-page or multi-page app (`index.html`, any frontend framework output)
- A static file host (Netlify, Vercel, GitHub Pages, Firebase Hosting, etc.)

Example Project Structure

```
dist/
├── index.html
├── main.js
├── pkg/
│    ├── my_app_bg.wasm
│    ├── my_app.js
│    ├── my_app.d.ts
```

Deploying to Netlify

1. Build your app and copy everything into `dist/`
2. Create a `netlify.toml`:

```
[build]

  publish = "dist"
```

3. Deploy:

```
npm install -g netlify-cli

netlify deploy --prod
```

Netlify serves your `.wasm` file with correct MIME types (`application/wasm`) and enables HTTP/2 for better load performance.

Deploying to GitHub Pages

```
npx gh-pages -d dist
```

This pushes the contents of the `dist/` directory to the `gh-pages` branch. GitHub Pages will serve the files directly at `https://<username>.github.io/<repo-name>/`.

CDN Hosting

If your WebAssembly binary is a standalone utility, a shared library, or a dependency consumed by multiple applications, using a CDN is more efficient and scalable.

CDNs cache files geographically and reduce latency by serving the asset from a node close to the user.

Good Candidates for CDN Hosting

- A WebAssembly image processing library
- A `.wasm` module compiled and shared via npm
- A binary used as part of a dynamic frontend loader

Hosting on Cloudflare R2 + Cloudflare CDN

1. Upload your `.wasm` binary to R2 using the Cloudflare dashboard or API.
2. Enable "public read access".
3. Serve with custom caching headers:

```
Content-Type: application/wasm

Cache-Control: public, max-age=31536000, immutable

Content-Encoding: gzip
```

4. Load the module in your app using **`WebAssembly.instantiateStreaming()`**:

```
const response = await
fetch('https://cdn.example.com/my_module_bg.wasm');
const wasmModule = await
WebAssembly.instantiateStreaming(response, {});
```

This approach ensures you're shipping a compressed, cacheable binary that can be shared across many apps without rebuilding.

Serverless WebAssembly

For use cases that involve computation rather than static delivery—such as transformation, validation, or business logic—you can run Rust-Wasm in a serverless function or edge compute environment.

This pushes your Wasm logic **close to the user**, executed on demand with no backend server required.

Use Cases

- On-the-fly Markdown to HTML rendering
- Signature verification or hashing
- Secure evaluation of user input (e.g., calculators, data validators)
- Audio or image processing before streaming

Cloudflare Workers (Edge Compute)

Cloudflare Workers support WebAssembly out of the box.

1. Install the CLI:

```
npm install -g wrangler
```

2. Configure `wrangler.toml`:

```
name = "markdown-worker"
type = "javascript"

[build]
command = "wasm-pack build --target no-modules"
```

3. In your Worker:

```
import wasm from './pkg/my_app_bg.wasm';

addEventListener('fetch', event => {
  event.respondWith(handle(event.request));
});

async function handle(request) {
```

```
  const { instance } = await
WebAssembly.instantiate(wasm);
  const result =
instance.exports.compute_something(42);
  return new Response(`Wasm computed: ${result}`);
}
```

4. Deploy:

```
wrangler publish
```

This gives you a globally distributed compute layer powered by your Rust code.

Vercel Edge Functions

Vercel supports Wasm in edge functions (in beta at the time of writing). Use the `WebAssembly.instantiate()` method inside a Vercel function to execute logic per request.

Key Hosting Considerations

Hosting Type	Use Case	Strengths	Tradeoffs
Static Site	Frontend apps, single-page applications	Simple, free tiers, no servers	No backend logic
CDN	Shared .wasm libraries, performance modules	Fast, cacheable, globally replicated	Requires versioning, immutable URLs
Serverless	Dynamic, request-based logic (e.g., image resize)	Runs anywhere, scales instantly	Cold starts, limited execution time

Serving .wasm Correctly

Regardless of host, always serve .wasm files with:

*   **Content-Type: application/wasm**
*   **Content-Encoding: gzip** or **br**

- **Cache-Control: public, max-age=31536000, immutable**

These headers ensure browsers treat `.wasm` correctly, cache it efficiently, and avoid unnecessary re-downloads on future visits.

Choosing the right hosting strategy depends on how your Rust-Wasm module is used:

- For apps with a UI, static hosting is fast and easy to manage.
- For reusable libraries, CDNs let you share and cache `.wasm` efficiently.
- For compute-heavy functions or real-time transformation, serverless platforms like Cloudflare Workers enable WebAssembly to run securely at the edge.

By aligning your hosting method with your application's needs, you can ship WebAssembly-powered experiences that are fast, efficient, and production-ready.

Best Practices for Loading and Caching WebAssembly (Wasm)

When deploying a WebAssembly module to production, your success depends not just on how well the code works, but on how **efficiently** it loads and runs in the browser. WebAssembly offers native-level speed, but the `.wasm` binary is a static resource that must be downloaded, parsed, compiled, and instantiated before it can execute. If you're not careful, your application will suffer from slow startup times, large binary downloads, or broken behavior due to caching issues.

Use `wasm-pack` and Target the Right Output

Start with a clean and optimized build:

```
wasm-pack build --target web --release
```

- The `--target web` option creates ES module bindings suitable for browsers.
- The `--release` flag ensures maximum code optimizations.
- The output appears in `pkg/`, ready for consumption.

You now have two key files:

- A `.wasm` file (your compiled logic)
- A `.js` loader file (generated wrapper)

These files work together to bootstrap your Wasm module inside a JavaScript environment.

Use Lazy Initialization to Control When Wasm Loads

Avoid loading Wasm modules at the top of your application unless absolutely necessary. Instead, load them **on demand**, just before they're needed.

```
import init, { parse_markdown } from
"./pkg/markdown_toolkit.js";

let wasmReady = false;

async function render() {
  if (!wasmReady) {
    await init(); // Loads and instantiates the
wasm file
    wasmReady = true;
  }

  const raw =
document.querySelector("#editor").value;
  const html = parse_markdown(raw);
  document.querySelector("#output").innerHTML =
html;
}
```

This pattern ensures that the `.wasm` binary is not fetched or compiled until the user actually triggers the functionality that needs it (e.g. clicking a "Render" button).

Compress the `.wasm` Binary with Gzip or Brotli

By default, WebAssembly files are not small. Even optimized `.wasm` files can range between 50 KB and 500 KB uncompressed. You should always serve a **compressed** version using either Gzip or Brotli.

Generate compressed files during deployment:

```
gzip -k -9 pkg/markdown_toolkit_bg.wasm

brotli -Z pkg/markdown_toolkit_bg.wasm
```

- `-k` keeps the original file
- `-9` or `-z` uses maximum compression level

Configure your server to serve compressed `.wasm` files:

For **Nginx**:

```
location ~* \.wasm$ {
    add_header Content-Type application/wasm;
    gzip_static on;
    brotli_static on;
    add_header Cache-Control "public, max-age=31536000, immutable";
}
```

For **Netlify**, add `_headers` in your `dist/` directory:

```
/pkg/*.wasm
  Content-Type: application/wasm
  Content-Encoding: br
  Cache-Control: public, max-age=31536000, immutable
```

Compressed Wasm reduces download time significantly without affecting performance.

Use `wasm-opt` to Strip Unused Code and Shrink Binary Size

Install **wasm-opt** (part of the Binaryen toolkit):

```
wasm-opt -Oz -o pkg/markdown_toolkit_bg.wasm pkg/markdown_toolkit_bg.wasm
```

- `-Oz` aggressively optimizes for size.
- Combine with `wee_alloc` in Rust for reduced allocator footprint.

In `Cargo.toml`:

```
[dependencies]
wee_alloc = "0.4"

[lib]
crate-type = ["cdylib"]

[profile.release]
opt-level = "z"
lto = true
codegen-units = 1
```

This setup minimizes the `.wasm` binary while keeping performance acceptable.

Use `instantiateStreaming` When Hosting `.wasm` Separately

When serving the `.wasm` file directly (not bundled into the JS), you can reduce startup time using **streaming compilation**:

```
const importObject = {};
const wasmModule = await
WebAssembly.instantiateStreaming(
  fetch("/pkg/markdown_toolkit_bg.wasm"),
  importObject
);
```

This allows the browser to **compile the binary while it's still downloading**, improving time-to-execution. Make sure:

- You serve with `Content-Type: application/wasm`
- You don't use Gzip unless your server supports **streamed decompression** (most modern hosts do)

Apply Long-Term Caching with Hash-Based Filenames

To take full advantage of CDN and browser caching, version your Wasm files using **content hashes**.

Example filename after build:

```
markdown_toolkit_bg.ab1d23ef.wasm
```

Update the JS loader to reference the new name:

```
import init from
'./pkg/markdown_toolkit_bg.ab1d23ef.wasm';
```

This lets you use aggressive caching:

```
Cache-Control: public, max-age=31536000, immutable
```

When you update the file, the hash changes and forces the browser to re-download it—without manual intervention.

Preload or Prefetch When Necessary

If you **know** your Wasm module will be needed soon (e.g. after the user logs in), you can preload or prefetch it to reduce latency.

In your HTML:

```
<link rel="preload"
href="/pkg/markdown_toolkit_bg.wasm" as="fetch"
type="application/wasm" crossorigin="anonymous">
```

Or for future use (non-blocking):

```
<link rel="prefetch"
href="/pkg/markdown_toolkit_bg.wasm" as="fetch">
```

This hints to the browser to begin fetching the file ahead of time without executing it immediately.

Avoid Blocking Main Thread on Wasm Compilation

WebAssembly compilation is fast—but not free. If your module is large, compile and instantiate it off the main thread using a Web Worker.

Example in main script:

```
const worker = new Worker("wasm-loader.js");
```

```
worker.onmessage = (e) => {
  const { result } = e.data;
  console.log("Wasm initialized:", result);
};
```

And in `wasm-loader.js`:

```
importScripts("pkg/markdown_toolkit.js");

(async () => {
  await init();
  postMessage({ result: "ready" });
})();
```

This ensures that UI rendering stays responsive while the Wasm runtime loads.

To deliver WebAssembly effectively in production, treat it like any other performance-critical asset:

- Compress it using Gzip or Brotli.
- Optimize the binary using `wasm-opt` and memory-efficient allocators.
- Cache it aggressively with hashed filenames and immutable cache headers.
- Lazy-load or stream-load Wasm to reduce startup costs.
- Offload compilation to a worker if the file is large or initialization is expensive.
- Use long-term caching strategies but always plan for cache busting via file hashes.

When combined, these best practices make your Rust-Wasm applications as fast and reliable to load as native JavaScript—while preserving the performance and safety benefits of Rust itself.

CI/CD Pipelines for Rust-Wasm Workflows

Continuous Integration and Continuous Deployment (CI/CD) are critical components of any modern development workflow—especially when you're building applications with multiple build targets like Rust, WebAssembly, JavaScript, and HTML. For Rust-Wasm projects, a well-structured pipeline ensures your application is built, tested, optimized, and deployed reliably with every change you push.

Because WebAssembly is a binary target, minor changes in Rust code can break the interface between Rust and JavaScript. CI pipelines help you detect these problems immediately, run tests in real browser environments, and enforce build consistency.

In addition, your `.wasm` binary should be:

- Built in release mode
- Optimized using `wasm-opt`
- Served with appropriate MIME and cache settings
- Versioned and deployed to your hosting platform

All of this benefits from automation.

Required Tools

- `wasm-pack` – to compile Rust into WebAssembly and generate JS bindings
- `wasm-bindgen-test` – to run unit tests for Wasm-targeted code
- `wasm-opt` – for size optimization
- **GitHub Actions** (or other CI platforms like GitLab CI, CircleCI)
- Hosting provider: GitHub Pages, Netlify, Vercel, or npm

CI Workflow Overview

Here's what your CI pipeline should do:

1. Check out the repository
2. Install Rust toolchain and wasm-pack
3. Build the Wasm module
4. Run tests in Node or headless browser
5. Optimize the Wasm output
6. Deploy to your target host or publish to npm

Example: GitHub Actions Workflow for Rust-Wasm

Create a file at `.github/workflows/wasm-build.yml`:

```
name: Build and Deploy Rust-Wasm

on:
```

```yaml
  push:
    branches:
      - main
  pull_request:
    branches:
      - main

jobs:
  build-test-deploy:
    runs-on: ubuntu-latest

    steps:
      - name: Check out code
        uses: actions/checkout@v3

      - name: Set up Rust
        uses: actions-rs/toolchain@v1
        with:
          toolchain: stable
          override: true

      - name: Install wasm-pack
        run: cargo install wasm-pack

      - name: Build Wasm Package
        run: wasm-pack build --release --target web

      - name: Run Wasm Tests
        run: wasm-pack test --headless --firefox

      - name: Install Binaryen (wasm-opt)
        run: |
          curl -LO
https://github.com/WebAssembly/binaryen/releases/do
wnload/version_114/binaryen-version_114-x86_64-
linux.tar.gz
          tar -xzf binaryen-version_114-x86_64-
linux.tar.gz
          sudo mv binaryen-version_114/bin/wasm-opt
/usr/local/bin

      - name: Optimize Wasm Output
```

```
        run: |
          wasm-opt -Oz -o pkg/your_crate_bg.wasm
pkg/your_crate_bg.wasm

      - name: Deploy to GitHub Pages
        uses: peaceiris/actions-gh-pages@v3
        with:
          github_token: ${{ secrets.GITHUB_TOKEN }}
          publish_dir: ./dist
```

Notes on Key Steps

```
wasm-pack build --release --target web
```

This compiles your Rust crate into WebAssembly and generates a JS module. `--target web` ensures compatibility with ES modules in browsers.

```
wasm-pack test --headless --firefox
```

This runs all unit tests using `wasm-bindgen-test`, inside a real browser. You can replace `--firefox` with `--chrome` or use `--node` for simpler logic tests.

wasm-opt -Oz

This strips dead code and compresses the output. It's crucial for reducing load times in production.

peaceiris/actions-gh-pages

This action pushes your `dist/` directory to a GitHub Pages branch. For Netlify or Vercel, you'd commit the build and use their CLI or deploy hook instead.

Publishing to npm

If you're distributing your crate as a reusable npm module (e.g. a Markdown parser, encoder, or validator), automate it like this:

```
      - name: Publish to npm
        if: github.ref == 'refs/heads/main'
        run: |
          cd pkg
          npm publish --access public
```

```
    env:
        NODE_AUTH_TOKEN: ${{ secrets.NPM_TOKEN }}
```

- Add NPM_TOKEN as a secret in your GitHub repo
- Make sure pkg/package.json has a unique and valid name
- Optionally use <u>semantic-release</u> for automated versioning

Real World Example: Deploying to Netlify

If your dist/ folder contains an SPA that depends on Wasm:

- **Add a `netlify.toml`:**

```
[build]
  publish = "dist"
  command = "wasm-pack build --release --target web
&& npm run build"
```

- In your GitHub Action, instead of using gh-pages, use:

```
    - name: Deploy to Netlify
      run: npx netlify deploy --dir=dist --prod
      env:
        NETLIFY_AUTH_TOKEN: ${{
secrets.NETLIFY_AUTH_TOKEN }}
        NETLIFY_SITE_ID: ${{
secrets.NETLIFY_SITE_ID }}
```

This pushes the site live whenever you commit to main.

Optional Enhancements

- Linting your Rust and JavaScript code before build
- Bundle analysis using tools like webpack-bundle-analyzer
- Automated benchmarking with size thresholds for .wasm files
- Testing multiple browsers in parallel

Using tools like GitHub Actions and wasm-pack, you can build, test, optimize, and deploy your Rust-Wasm project on every push—whether it's a user-facing web app or a shared module distributed via npm. This gives you the same level of rigor, automation, and safety you'd expect from any mature frontend or backend system.

Chapter 10: Beyond the Browser: WASI and Server-Side WebAssembly

Up until this point, we've focused on running Rust-compiled WebAssembly inside the browser. But WebAssembly's potential is not limited to frontend use. Thanks to the WebAssembly System Interface (WASI) and modern runtimes like Wasmtime, Wasmer, and support in edge platforms like Cloudflare Workers, WebAssembly is expanding into server-side applications, desktop environments, and even embedded systems.

This chapter explores how WebAssembly can be used **outside the browser—** running secure, fast, and portable code across platforms. You'll learn how to build and run Rust-Wasm modules on the server, integrate with edge computing platforms, and even package them into native desktop apps. Finally, we'll look ahead at how WebAssembly is shaping the future of cross-platform application development.

Introduction to WASI (WebAssembly System Interface)

WebAssembly was originally designed as a portable runtime for executing code securely in web browsers. Its core features—sandboxing, fast startup, and compact binaries—made it ideal for frontend applications. However, running WebAssembly outside the browser presented a limitation: it lacked a standard way to interact with the host system. That's where **WASI**, the *WebAssembly System Interface*, comes in.

WASI provides a standardized set of APIs that allow WebAssembly modules to perform basic system-level operations such as reading files, writing output, handling clocks, accessing environment variables, and more—without giving up the security guarantees that WebAssembly was built on. It acts as a bridge between Wasm modules and the operating system in a way that is both safe and portable.

WASI is a modular system interface for WebAssembly programs, designed by the Bytecode Alliance. It gives WebAssembly access to operating system features in a secure and capability-based manner.

WASI does **not** expose the full functionality of a traditional operating system. Instead, it focuses on essential capabilities like:

- File system I/O
- Standard input/output (stdin, stdout, stderr)
- Environment variables
- High-resolution clocks
- Random number generation

This limited, but well-defined API surface makes WASI ideal for use cases where security, portability, and performance are important—such as plugins, command-line tools, and sandboxed execution environments.

Why WASI Matters

Without WASI, WebAssembly modules outside the browser have no built-in way to perform basic tasks like printing to the terminal or accessing files. These operations are possible only if the host runtime provides custom APIs, which limits portability and creates tight coupling between modules and their hosts.

WASI solves this by offering a **standardized interface**. This means you can:

- Compile a Rust program to WebAssembly with WASI support.
- Run that module on any WASI-compliant runtime (such as Wasmtime, Wasmer, or Node.js with experimental support).
- Expect the same behavior across platforms—Linux, macOS, Windows, and even embedded systems.

WASI's Capability-Based Security Model

One of WASI's defining features is **capability-based security**. This means that a WebAssembly module can only access the resources it is explicitly given. For example, it cannot read or write arbitrary files on the host system unless the host grants it access to specific directories.

This is different from traditional native applications, which inherit broad access to system resources. In WASI, the module must be granted capabilities (e.g., access to `/tmp/data`), and the host enforces those boundaries strictly.

This model improves safety, especially when executing untrusted code or running multiple modules in isolation.

How WASI Works in Practice (Using Rust)

You can build a command-line-like application in Rust, compile it to WebAssembly with WASI support, and run it using a WASI-compatible runtime like Wasmtime.

Example Rust Code

```
use std::io::{self, Write};

fn main() {
    let mut input = String::new();
    println!("Enter your name:");
    io::stdin().read_line(&mut input).unwrap();
    writeln!(io::stdout(), "Hello, {}!",
input.trim()).unwrap();
}
```

This program reads from stdin and writes to stdout—basic I/O that depends on system access.

Compile to WASI target

```
rustup target add wasm32-wasi

cargo build --target wasm32-wasi --release
```

The output will be a .wasm file located at:

```
target/wasm32-wasi/release/your_binary.wasm
```

Run the WASM file with Wasmtime

```
wasmtime target/wasm32-
wasi/release/your_binary.wasm
```

You can now interact with the module as if it were a native executable.

WASI-Compatible Runtimes

Several runtimes support executing WASI modules, each with their own focus:

- **Wasmtime**: A lightweight, production-ready runtime created by the Bytecode Alliance.
- **Wasmer**: A runtime with multi-language support and a plugin system for extending functionality.
- **Node.js**: Experimental WASI support via the `--experimental-wasi-unstable-preview1` flag.
- **Spin**: A developer-friendly framework by Fermyon for deploying Wasm functions as services.

These runtimes allow you to build secure, language-agnostic server-side applications or tools that run anywhere WebAssembly is supported.

Limitations and Evolving Features

As of today, WASI is still evolving. The current stable version (WASI Preview 1) supports a minimal set of capabilities. Many features you might expect from a full OS API—like sockets, dynamic libraries, or threads—are not yet stable.

However, development is active, and proposals like **WASI sockets**, **WASI HTTP**, and **WASI filesystem improvements** are making their way through the WebAssembly standards process. These will eventually allow developers to write full-featured backend services, servers, and even multi-threaded applications using Wasm and Rust.

WASI extends WebAssembly beyond the browser by enabling safe and portable system-level capabilities. It makes it possible to write applications in Rust (and other languages), compile them to WebAssembly, and run them in sandboxed environments with controlled access to system resources.

With WASI, you can:

- Build secure CLI tools and utilities in Rust
- Run Wasm modules on the server or edge with file and environment access
- Reuse code across frontend, backend, and native platforms

This is a major step toward making WebAssembly a true cross-platform application runtime—and Rust is one of the best languages for taking full advantage of it.

Running Rust-Wasm on the Backend

WebAssembly was originally built for running code securely in web browsers, but its design also makes it suitable for server-side environments. On the backend, WebAssembly can run Rust code with strong sandboxing, fast startup times, and cross-platform portability. Whether you're deploying to edge computing platforms like **Cloudflare Workers** or using general-purpose Wasm runtimes like **Wasmtime**, you can execute Rust-compiled WebAssembly modules efficiently and safely outside the browser.

Why Run WebAssembly on the Backend?

WebAssembly has several properties that make it valuable on the server:

- **Portability**: A `.wasm` file can run on any platform with a compatible runtime.
- **Security**: Wasm modules execute in a sandbox and cannot access system resources unless explicitly permitted.
- **Fast startup**: Wasm binaries load and initialize more quickly than containers or VMs.
- **Multi-language support**: Code written in different languages can be compiled to Wasm and run together in a shared environment.

Running Rust-Wasm on the backend allows you to take advantage of these characteristics in serverless platforms, microservices, plugin systems, or command-line tools.

Using Wasmtime to Run Rust-Wasm Modules

Wasmtime is a lightweight and efficient WebAssembly runtime developed by the Bytecode Alliance. It supports the WASI (WebAssembly System Interface) specification, which allows WebAssembly modules to perform system-like tasks (e.g., file I/O, reading environment variables, etc.) in a controlled manner.

Step 1: Create a Simple Rust Program

Here's a Rust program that adds two numbers:

```
use wasm_bindgen::prelude::*;

#[wasm_bindgen]
pub fn add(a: i32, b: i32) -> i32 {
    a + b
}
```

If you want to use WASI features (e.g., file access or stdin/stdout), write a standard `fn main()` application instead:

```
fn main() {
    println!("Hello from WASI!");
}
```

Step 2: Compile for WebAssembly

For WASI-compatible Rust code:

```
rustup target add wasm32-wasi
cargo build --target wasm32-wasi --release
```

This produces a `.wasm` file in `target/wasm32-wasi/release/your_app.wasm`.

Step 3: Install and Use Wasmtime

Install Wasmtime using your package manager or the prebuilt binary:

curl https://wasmtime.dev/install.sh -sSf | bash

Run the `.wasm` file with:

```
wasmtime target/wasm32-wasi/release/your_app.wasm
```

Wasmtime executes the WebAssembly module just like a native binary—but in a secure, sandboxed context.

You can also embed Wasmtime into your own host application (written in Rust or C) to load and run Wasm modules dynamically.

Using Cloudflare Workers for Edge Deployment

178

Cloudflare Workers is a serverless platform that runs lightweight scripts close to the user (at the edge). It supports executing Wasm modules alongside JavaScript logic in a fast, low-latency environment.

Cloudflare Workers do not support WASI but can execute WebAssembly that does not require file I/O or system access.

Step 1: Build Your Rust-Wasm Module

Use `wasm-pack` to compile your Rust code to a format suitable for Workers:

```
wasm-pack build --target no-modules --release
```

This generates:

- A `.wasm` binary
- A JS wrapper that can load and call the module

Step 2: Set Up a Worker with Wrangler

Install the Wrangler CLI:

```
npm install -g wrangler
```

Create a new project:

```
wrangler init rust-wasm-worker
cd rust-wasm-worker
```

Add your generated `.wasm` and JS files into the `./pkg` directory.

Step 3: Write the Worker Code

In `index.js`:

```
import wasm from './pkg/your_module_bg.wasm';

addEventListener('fetch', event => {
  event.respondWith(handleRequest(event.request));
});

async function handleRequest(request) {
```

```
  const { instance } = await
WebAssembly.instantiate(wasm);
  const result = instance.exports.add(5, 7);
  return new Response(`5 + 7 = ${result}`);
}
```

This loads and runs the add function from your compiled Rust-Wasm module.

Step 4: Deploy to Cloudflare

In `wrangler.toml`:

```
name = "rust-wasm-worker"

type = "javascript"

account_id = "your_account_id"

workers_dev = true
```

Deploy with:

```
wrangler publish
```

Your Wasm-powered Worker is now live at a Cloudflare-provided URL and running at the edge in data centers worldwide.

Key Differences Between Wasmtime and Cloudflare Workers

Feature	Wasmtime	Cloudflare Workers
WASI support	☑ Full	✖ Not supported
File system access	☑ Via WASI	✖ Not allowed
Suitable for long tasks	☑ Yes (native runtime)	✖ Short-lived execution only
Edge deployment	✖ No	☑ Global network
Runtime environment	Standalone binary or embedded	V8 isolate (JavaScript + Wasm)
Use case	CLI tools, server-side logic	Fast edge APIs, low-latency scripts

Practical Use Cases

Wasmtime:

- Secure plugin systems (e.g., executing third-party logic safely)
- Lightweight CLI tools compiled to `.wasm`
- Running Wasm in containers or microservices with limited permissions

Cloudflare Workers:

- Input validation and transformation at the edge
- Markdown or JSON parsing using Rust-Wasm
- CPU-bound tasks where latency matters (e.g., UUID generation, encoding)

Running Rust-Wasm on the backend allows you to bring Rust's safety and performance to modern, scalable execution environments:

- **Wasmtime** provides a full-featured runtime with WASI support for building CLI tools, microservices, and embedded Wasm engines.
- **Cloudflare Workers** let you deploy lightweight Rust-Wasm modules globally, optimized for edge computing with fast response times and low resource usage.

These tools expand the use of WebAssembly far beyond frontend code, enabling secure, portable, and efficient backend systems powered by Rust.

Tauri and Cross-Platform Desktop Apps

Tauri is a modern framework for building lightweight, secure, and cross-platform desktop applications using web technologies like HTML, CSS, and JavaScript for the frontend, and Rust for the backend. It provides a developer-friendly structure that allows you to create native desktop apps while maintaining the performance, security, and small binary size that Rust is known for.

Tauri is an open-source toolkit for building desktop applications that use a **WebView** (such as WebKit or Windows WebView2) to render a web frontend, and a **Rust backend** to handle native functionality.

Unlike Electron, which packages a full Chromium engine with each app (resulting in large binaries), Tauri uses the native WebView component provided by the operating system. This significantly reduces application size and memory usage.

Key features:

- Small binary size (typically under 5MB)
- Strong sandboxing and security controls
- First-class Rust integration
- Native APIs for file access, notifications, clipboard, etc.
- Windows, macOS, and Linux support

Tauri + Rust-Wasm: A Practical Integration

Although Tauri applications already use Rust for backend logic, you can also use Rust-Wasm **inside the frontend**, especially for tasks that require performance, safety, or code reuse across platforms.

This setup allows you to:

- Run Rust logic inside the WebView as a WebAssembly module
- Use the same `.wasm` module in a browser-based version of your app
- Offload compute-heavy or secure tasks to Wasm instead of relying on JavaScript

Example Use Case: Markdown Parser in Tauri with Rust-Wasm

Step 1: Create a Tauri Project

Install the required tools:

```
npm create tauri-app

cd my-tauri-app
```

This sets up a basic project with a frontend in your chosen framework (e.g., vanilla JS, React, Svelte) and a Rust-based backend.

Step 2: Add a Rust-Wasm Module

Create a separate Rust crate (you can place it in a `wasm/` directory):

```
cargo new --lib markdown_parser

cd markdown_parser
```

In Cargo.toml:

```
[lib]
crate-type = ["cdylib"]

[dependencies]
wasm-bindgen = "0.2"
```

In `src/lib.rs`:

```
use wasm_bindgen::prelude::*;

#[wasm_bindgen]
pub fn render_markdown(input: &str) -> String {
    markdown::to_html(input)
}
```

Use a library like `pulldown-cmark` or your own implementation to parse Markdown.

Step 3: Build with wasm-pack

Install `wasm-pack` if you haven't already:

```
cargo install wasm-pack
```

Then build the module:

```
wasm-pack build --target bundler --out-dir ../src-tauri/wasm_pkg
```

This outputs a `.wasm` file and JS bindings you can use in your frontend.

Step 4: Use in Your Frontend Code

In your Tauri frontend (e.g., inside a React component):

```
import init, { render_markdown } from
"./wasm_pkg/markdown_parser";

async function renderPreview() {
  await init(); // Initialize the Wasm module
  const input = "# Hello from Rust-Wasm";
  const output = render_markdown(input);
  document.getElementById("preview").innerHTML =
output;
}
```

This renders Markdown directly in the frontend, using Rust-Wasm for parsing.

Benefits of Using Rust-Wasm in Tauri Apps

- **Code reuse**: You can use the same `.wasm` module in your web app and your desktop app.
- **Performance**: Rust outperforms JavaScript for many algorithms and data processing tasks.
- **Security**: Wasm runs in a sandboxed environment and can safely execute untrusted logic.
- **Maintainability**: You can write critical logic in Rust while using familiar tools for the frontend.

When to Use Rust-Wasm vs. Tauri Backend Commands

Tauri allows two main forms of Rust integration:

- **Tauri commands**: These are native Rust functions called from the frontend via IPC (inter-process communication). Use these when you need full OS access (e.g., file system, networking).
- **Rust-Wasm**: Runs in the frontend WebView sandbox. Use this when you want to execute pure, CPU-bound Rust logic without crossing the IPC boundary.

You can even combine both: use Wasm for data transformation, and Tauri commands for accessing the file system or shell.

Limitations to Consider

- WebAssembly does not have access to OS APIs unless explicitly bridged (e.g., through Tauri backend commands).
- Communication between frontend JS and Wasm can be more complex for large or structured data unless you use `serde` + `wasm-bindgen`.
- For UI-level interactions, it may be easier to stick with JavaScript unless performance is a concern.

Tauri gives you a powerful foundation for building secure, fast, and cross-platform desktop apps. By combining Tauri with Rust-Wasm, you can:

- Build desktop apps that use Rust not only for the backend but also for frontend logic
- Reuse your Wasm code across web and native applications
- Take advantage of WebAssembly's performance and sandboxing in a modern desktop setting

This approach is well-suited for developers who want to build fast, maintainable applications using the best of both web and native technologies.

The Future of WebAssembly Beyond Frontend

WebAssembly (Wasm) began as a technology for running high-performance code safely inside web browsers, but it has grown into a broader execution format with uses well beyond the browser. The same qualities that made it appealing for web use—speed, safety, portability, and compact size—also make it a strong candidate for server-side applications, embedded systems, plugin architectures, and distributed computing.

At its core, WebAssembly is a **portable binary instruction format**. Code written in languages like Rust, C, C++, or AssemblyScript can be compiled to Wasm and executed in any environment that supports the WebAssembly runtime specification.

Because Wasm is platform-agnostic and sandboxed, it avoids many of the compatibility and security concerns associated with native code. This positions WebAssembly as a **universal runtime**—a consistent way to execute code across operating systems, devices, and architectures.

Evolving Use Cases Beyond the Browser

While WebAssembly started in browsers, developers and infrastructure providers are now applying it in new ways:

1. Server-Side Applications

With runtimes like **Wasmtime**, **Wasmer**, and **WasmEdge**, developers can run WebAssembly modules on the server, often alongside or in place of traditional services.

Benefits include:

- Faster startup than containers
- Resource isolation without full virtualization
- Easier multi-language integration
- Safe execution of third-party or untrusted code

WebAssembly modules are being used to power microservices, APIs, and serverless functions where fast execution and strong isolation are critical.

2. Edge Computing

Platforms such as **Cloudflare Workers**, **Fastly Compute@Edge**, and **Fermyon Spin** enable WebAssembly modules to run at the edge—close to users, in globally distributed data centers.

This supports low-latency processing for:

- Content transformation
- Personalized responses
- Security filtering
- Request validation

Because Wasm modules are compact and quick to start, they are ideal for executing workloads on-demand in edge locations.

3. Plugin Systems

Applications that need to load and run third-party code safely are adopting WebAssembly for extensibility.

Examples:

- Graphics engines embedding Wasm plugins for shaders or asset processing
- Game engines using Wasm for mod support
- Tools like **Envoy Proxy** using Wasm for user-defined filters
- Databases embedding Wasm for custom logic (e.g., SQLite extensions)

Wasm ensures that user plugins can't crash or compromise the host system, thanks to its sandboxed execution model.

4. Desktop and Mobile Applications

WebAssembly is also showing up in **desktop apps** via frameworks like **Tauri**, which use Wasm in the frontend, and in mobile tools that embed Wasm modules for cross-platform logic.

This allows developers to write core logic once (in Rust or another language), compile it to WebAssembly, and reuse it across web, desktop, and mobile interfaces.

WASI and System-Level Access

To enable server-side and system-level capabilities, the WebAssembly community is building **WASI**—the WebAssembly System Interface.

WASI defines APIs for performing:

- File and directory I/O
- Network access
- Time and clock operations
- Process management
- Random number generation

WASI is evolving to support more features commonly used by native applications, with an emphasis on sandboxing and capability-based security. This allows WebAssembly to gradually take on roles traditionally reserved for native binaries.

Component Model and Module Interoperability

One of the most significant developments for WebAssembly is the **Component Model**.

This model aims to:

- Allow Wasm modules compiled from different languages to communicate seamlessly
- Support richer type information across module boundaries
- Enable reusable, composable Wasm libraries and packages

With the Component Model, a Rust-based Wasm module could call a module written in C or Go, exchange structured data, and be composed into larger systems—all without complex glue code or unsafe bindings.

Upcoming Features in WebAssembly

The WebAssembly specification continues to expand. Upcoming proposals include:

- **Threads**: Support for multithreading using shared memory (enabled with `wasm-threads`)
- **Exception Handling**: Structured error handling without relying on host traps
- **Garbage Collection**: Enabling languages like Java, Kotlin, or C# to compile efficiently to Wasm
- **Tail Calls and SIMD**: Enhancing performance for compute-heavy applications

These additions make WebAssembly more capable as a general-purpose runtime.

WebAssembly in Production: Real-World Examples

- **Shopify** uses Wasm to sandbox extensions safely in their e-commerce platform.
- **Figma** uses Wasm in the browser to enable fast graphics editing in a collaborative environment.
- **Bytecode Alliance** is building foundational tools and standards to support secure Wasm execution across devices.
- **Docker** now supports running WebAssembly modules as a container alternative with WASI runtimes.

WebAssembly is moving far beyond frontend development. With the support of WASI, advanced runtimes, and an expanding feature set, Wasm is becoming a standard for secure, fast, and portable code execution across environments:

- On the **server**, it's replacing scripts and containers for microservices.
- At the **edge**, it's powering scalable, low-latency computing.
- In **apps**, it's improving performance and portability.
- As a **plugin engine**, it's enabling extensibility with strict isolation.

Rust plays a key role in this ecosystem due to its Wasm-first tooling, memory safety, and performance. As the WebAssembly standard grows, developers who understand how to compile, run, and optimize Rust for Wasm will be well-positioned to build applications that run anywhere.

Appendices

The appendices in this book are designed to support your learning and reference needs as you work with Rust and WebAssembly. Whether you're troubleshooting an issue, recalling syntax, or exploring further tools and communities, these sections give you quick, reliable information to refer back to.

Appendix A: Rust Language Cheat Sheet

This cheat sheet summarizes key Rust syntax and concepts that are especially useful when working with WebAssembly.

Variables and Mutability

```
let x = 5;              // Immutable by default
let mut y = 10;         // Mutable
```

Functions

```
fn add(a: i32, b: i32) -> i32 {
    a + b
}
```

Control Flow

```
if x > 0 {
    println!("Positive");
} else {
    println!("Zero or negative");
}

for i in 0..5 {
    println!("{}", i);
}
```

Pattern Matching

```
match value {
    0 => println!("Zero"),
    1..=5 => println!("Between 1 and 5"),
```

```
    _ => println!("Something else"),
}
```

Structs and Enums

```
struct User {
    name: String,
    age: u32,
}

enum Status {
    Success,
    Error(String),
}
```

Ownership and Borrowing

```
fn greet(name: &str) {
    println!("Hello, {}", name);
}
```

Error Handling

```
fn safe_divide(a: i32, b: i32) -> Result<i32,
String> {
    if b == 0 {
        Err("Cannot divide by zero".into())
    } else {
        Ok(a / b)
    }
}
```

Appendix B: `wasm-bindgen` and `web-sys` Reference

wasm-bindgen is a Rust crate and tool that facilitates interaction between Rust-generated WebAssembly and JavaScript. It allows you to:

- Export Rust functions to JavaScript
- Import JavaScript APIs into Rust
- Handle type conversion across the Wasm boundary

Example: Exporting a function to JavaScript

```
use wasm_bindgen::prelude::*;

#[wasm_bindgen]
pub fn greet(name: &str) {
    web_sys::console::log_1(&format!("Hello, {}",
name).into());
}
```

Supported Export Types

- **i32, f64**
- **String**
- **bool**
- **JsValue**
- **Result<T, JsValue>**

Common Macros

- **#[wasm_bindgen]**: Marks functions/types for binding
- **#[wasm_bindgen(start)]**: Marks the entry point

web-sys provides bindings to native browser APIs, including the DOM, console, events, and more. It enables you to work directly with browser objects in Rust.

Example: Changing the document title

```
use web_sys::window;

pub fn set_title(title: &str) {
    let document =
window().unwrap().document().unwrap();
    document.set_title(title);
}
```

Useful Modules in **web-sys**

- window, document, Element, Event
- console::log_1, console::error_1
- HtmlCanvasElement, CanvasRenderingContext2d
- KeyboardEvent, MouseEvent

To use a browser API, enable the feature in `Cargo.toml`:

```
web-sys = { version = "0.3", features = ["console",
"Window", "Document"] }
```

Appendix C: Debugging and Troubleshooting

Common Issues and Fixes

1. **`wasm-bindgen` not exporting functions**

   Make sure functions are public and annotated with `#[wasm_bindgen]`.

```
#[wasm_bindgen]

pub fn compute() { /* ... */ }
```

2. **Cannot read property of undefined**

   Ensure you call the module's `init()` function before invoking any exports.

```
import init, { do_work } from './pkg/my_module.js';

await init();

do_work();
```

3. **Panic messages not showing**

   Add this line at startup to show panic messages in the browser console:

   `console_error_panic_hook::set_once();`

   Add the dependency:

   `console_error_panic_hook = "0.1"`

4. **No output from `println!()`**

   `println!` has no effect in browser contexts. Use `web_sys::console::log_1()` instead.

```
use web_sys::console;

console::log_1(&"Debug info".into());
```

5. **Missing features in `web-sys`**

   You must explicitly enable each API in `Cargo.toml`. For example:

   ```
   features = ["Window", "Document",
   "HtmlCanvasElement"]
   ```

Appendix D: Further Resources and Community Links

Official Documentation

- Rust: https://doc.rust-lang.org/
- wasm-bindgen: https://rustwasm.github.io/wasm-bindgen/
- WebAssembly: https://webassembly.org/
- WASI: https://github.com/WebAssembly/WASI
- web-sys: https://docs.rs/web-sys

Community and Support

- Rust Users Forum
- Rust Wasm Book
- GitHub Discussions
- WebAssembly Community Group
- The Bytecode Alliance

Helpful Tools

- `wasm-pack`: Tool to build and package Rust-Wasm modules
- `wasm-opt`: Optimizes `.wasm` binaries for size and speed
- `wasm-bindgen-test`: Runs unit tests in Wasm contexts
- `wasm-server-runner`: Simple static file server for local testing

These appendices are designed to make your development process smoother and more productive. Keep them nearby as you continue building with Rust and WebAssembly.

www.ingramcontent.com/pod-product-compliance
Lightning Source LLC
Chambersburg PA
CBHW080553060326
40689CB00021B/4843